Instructions for using AR

LET AUGMENTED REALITY CHANGE HOW YOU READ A BOOK

With your smartphone, iPad or tablet you can use the **Hasmark AR** app to invoke the augmented reality experience to literally read outside the book.

 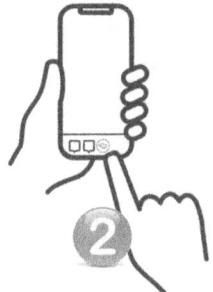 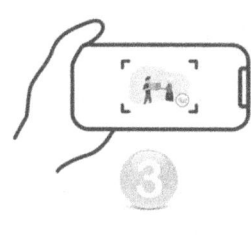

1. Download the **Hasmark app** from the **Apple App Store** or **Google Play**

2. Open and select the (vue) option

3. Point your lens at the full image with the and enjoy the augmented reality experience.

Go ahead and try it right now with the Hasmark Publishing International logo.

ENDORSEMENTS

"Naise Silapa's *The Deliberate Climb* is a profoundly moving and insightful journey through resilience and spiritual growth. Her compelling narrative and practical wisdom offer a beacon of hope and guidance for anyone seeking to transform life's challenges into stepping stones for success."

~ Peggy McColl, *New York Times* Bestselling Author
http://PeggyMcColl.com

"*The Deliberate Climb* is a powerful story of genuine self-discovery, courage, and perseverance. Naise's deliberate transformation has been an honor and inspiration to witness in real life. From her sitting in my lounge room, shakily asking me for funds to send to the man who had captured her heart, to the vulnerable, shaken woman who worked every waking hour to rebuild her shattered financial world, to her trembling yet deliberate step-by-step climb up the Q1, I watched Naise take conscious, intentional steps to rebuild her life, including writing this book so she could help empower other women. Thank you, Naise, for being such a wonderful beacon of hope, faith, and insight."

~ Michelle Lee,
Transformation and Life Coach

"In this book you will read about Naise and her deliberate climb. I describe it as a woman with amazing courage, resilience, and determination. Taking responsibility for oneself is a hard act to follow and being completely down and out shows me truly how incredible Naise is. Reading this book showed me no matter what struggle we are facing, there is always a solution. It is within us as individuals and by surrounding ourselves with people who support us. There is always a way!! Reading *The Deliberate Climb* will give you the strength to move forward, knowing you have the support of the author, Naise, and the tools to work on your life and your individual climb. Thank you, Naise, for your honesty, vulnerability, and incredible soul in writing this book. I'm sure you are helping more people than you know."

~ Shelly Langan,
The High Performance Mindset Coach
www.shelleylangan.com

"*The Deliberate Climb* is an inspiring and compelling transformational story with phenomenal life lessons that leave you with new ideas, success tips, faith, and growth. There are so many guidelines. Follow them and you will experience life with deliberate intention. This book shows a journey of not giving up and getting up no matter what. It is filled with the wisdom of some of the best personal growth masters, and it can absolutely serve as a light at the end of a tunnel when experiencing adversity or challenges. It is a page-turner and a must-read if you truly desire better results. Many people are raised to believe they are not the ones who can create success. Naise has shown the path of light, growth, and how one chooses to create a life worth living. I truly believe this book will enrich you!"

~Vladimira Kuna,
The Greatest Sales Chic on the Planet
and International Bestselling Author of
The Bible of the Masterminds and
In the Realm of the Magic Ruby

"The author, Naise, shows us by her real-life examples how to overcome life challenges and to summit the mountain to be happy and successful in this tremendous book! Inspirational!"

~ Dr. Mark Eric Wallace,
Tampa, Florida

"A compelling narrative of resilience, akin to steel forged in fire. This transformative journey from adversity to triumph exemplifies the power of mind over matter, making it essential reading for anyone seeking to overcome life's challenges."

~ Mila Lansdowne,
Personal and Business Development Coach

"*The Deliberate Climb* is a remarkable testament to Naise Silapa's beliefs and convictions, a true credit to her ability to express herself, and a generous contribution to the service of others. It's one of those books that call for repeated reading, especially for those who are facing life's seemingly insurmountable challenges."

~ Dr. Cassandra J. O'Loughlin,
Peer-reviewed and Published Academic Writer
and Author of *Taking My Breath*

"This enlightening book is a valuable resource for anyone seeking to overcome challenges and learn important lessons through extraordinary personal accounts shared within its pages. A powerful testimony of overcoming obstacles and providing a constructive and practical approach to transforming oneself, making it all the more insightful and worthwhile."

~ Shelly Southam Master,
Peace Life Coaching

"In the pages of *The Deliberate Climb*, we are invited into the raw, unvarnished truth of a woman who faced adversity on a scale many would find insurmountable. Her story, marked by the heartbreak of a marriage ending, the deceit of a romance scam, and the looming shadow of financial ruin, could easily have been one of defeat. Yet, it is anything but. This is a tale of unwavering courage, the kind that flourishes in the face of adversity, and a testament to the indomitable strength of a mother's love. Through her dedication to practices such as gratitude and intentional goal setting, the author not only navigates her way out of debt but also reclaims her life and spirit, all while raising her children single-handedly. It's a journey that speaks to the power of resilience, the importance of self-belief, and the transformative effect of gratitude and focused intention.

As someone who deeply values the power of self-improvement and the potential for personal transformation, even in our darkest moments, I was profoundly moved by the honesty and bravery of this story. *The Deliberate Climb* is not just a memoir; it is a beacon of hope for anyone who finds themselves facing seemingly insurmountable challenges. It reminds us all that with courage, determination, and a heart full of gratitude, it is possible to overcome the toughest of times and emerge stronger and more fulfilled on the other side. This book is a must-read for those who seek inspiration, for anyone who believes in the transformative power of personal resilience, and for all who have ever dared to dream of a brighter, more empowered future despite the odds. Let *The Deliberate Climb* be your guide on a journey of recovery, empowerment, and the ultimate triumph of the human spirit."

~ Georgia Clare

"Naise Silapa shares dark moments in her personal life in order to help the reader learn various techniques that we can use to recover from hardship in our lives. From meditation and reflection to living with gratitude and surrendering to that which we cannot change, The Deliberate Climb provides many excellent suggestions for processing grief, deception and loss."

~ Tressa Mitchener International Bestselling
Author of "Looking Out From the Inside"

"'The Deliberate Climb' provides the readers with a prism into what it takes to not just beat adversity and survive but to thrive. It is penned to help anyone who finds themselves in a heartbreaking circumstance, despite their culture, religion, social background, or education. No matter where you are in your journey, this book will be the inspiration you need in your corner. Great book and I highly recommend it!"

~ Dr. Honiara Amosa

"'The Deliberate Climb' offers hope to anyone who has ever been deceived by an online scammer or who has had to go through the difficulty of divorce and financial hardship. It offers many wonderful tips on how to reinvent yourself and bounce back stronger than ever before."

~ Judy O'Beirn
President of Hasmark Publishing International

THE DELIBERATE CLIMB

NAISE SILAPA

Published by
Hasmark Publishing International
www.hasmarkpublishing.com

Copyright © 2024 Naise Silapa
First Edition

No part of this book may be reproduced or transmitted in any form or by any means, electronic or mechanical, including photocopying, recording or by any information storage and retrieval system, without written permission from the author, except for the inclusion of brief quotations in a review.

Disclaimer

This book is designed to provide information and motivation to our readers. It is sold with the understanding that the publisher is not engaged to render any type of medical, psychological, legal, or any other kind of professional advice. The content of each article is the sole expression and opinion of its author, and not necessarily that of the publisher. No warranties or guarantees are expressed or implied by the publisher's choice to include any of the content in this volume. Neither the publisher nor the individual author shall be liable for any physical, psychological, emotional, financial, or commercial damages, including, but not limited to, special, incidental, consequential or other damages. Our views and rights are the same: You are responsible for your own choices, actions, and results.

Permission should be addressed in writing to Naise Silapa at nsilapa12@gmail.com.

Editor: Sigrid Macdonald (sigridmac13@hotmail.com)
Cover Design: Anne Karklins (anne@hasmarkpublishing.com)
Interior Layout: Amit Dey (amit@hasmarkpublishing.com)

ISBN 13: 978-1-77482-265-4
ISBN 10: 1-77482-265-2

DEDICATION

To my dear mother, Oloa, and grandmother, Vaitagata:

This book is a tribute to the two remarkable women who shaped my life with their strength, wisdom, and unconditional love. My mother, with her strength and grace, wove a fabric of inspiration through every challenge and triumph. My grandmother's nurturing spirit and guidance in my formative years provided a foundation of love and courage.

Both of you, from the shores of Samoa to the lessons echoed in my heart, continue to guide and inspire me. Your spirits live on—not just within the pages of this book, but in the lives you've profoundly touched and shaped.

I miss you both dearly.

With love, gratitude, and eternal respect,
Naise x

TABLE OF CONTENTS

Foreword By Hooligan Hefs xix
Introduction xxiii

Chapter 1   The Fall. 1
              The Inception of the Climb 1
              My Story. 2
              The Day Everything Changed 12
              The First Step to Rising. 16
              The Genesis of Proactive Transformation. . . . 19

Chapter 2   Spiritual Foundations 23
              A Return to Inner Peace 23
              Trusting God's Plan 25
              The Power of Surrender. 26
              Lessons in Faith and Resilience. 28
              Embracing Spiritual Growth 30

Chapter 3   Embracing the Lessons of the Past 33
              Island Roots: Life in Samoa's Embrace. 33
              Past as a Compass, not a Cage 35
              The Power of Reflection 36
              Embracing the Wisdom of Experience. 37

Chapter 4	Lessons from Bob Proctor 39
	The Genius Mind 39
	Creating a Personal Paradigm Shift 42
	Setting Boundaries and Goals 43
	Riding the Waves of Vibration............ 45
	Transforming Adversity into Achievement .. 47
Chapter 5	Mother, the Guiding Star 51
	The Foundations of Her Influence 51
	Maternal Memories 52
	Pearls of Wisdom 53
	A Mother's Eternal Influence 55
	The Anchor of Unwavering Belief 56
Chapter 6	Navigating Single Motherhood........ 59
	The Double Battle 59
	Celebrating Small Victories 60
	Reinventing the Meaning of Success........ 61
	Building Resilience for Two.............. 63
Chapter 7	Financial Rebuilding............... 65
	The Spiritual Side of Money 65
	Practical Steps to Cultivate a Wealth Mindset . 66
	Recognizing Money Mindset Blocks........ 67
	Strategies for Financial Recovery 68
	Building a Sustainable and Empowered Financial Future 71

Chapter 8 Deliberate Action and Transformation . 73
Harnessing the Power of Intention 73
The Power of Perspective 76
Small Actions, Monumental Changes. 78
The Art of Proactive Living 79

Chapter 9 Life's True Wealth 81
Valuing Non-Material Blessings 81
The Transformative Power of Gratitude 82
Nurturing Deep Connections. 83
The Abundance in Everyday Moments 85
Kindness & Empathy 86

Chapter 10 Embracing Order in Life 89
Find Order in Chaos 89
Mindfulness & Meditation 92
Foundations of Strength 95
Relationships and Boundaries. 97
Embracing Uncertainty with Structure 98

Chapter 11 Emotional Resilience. 101
Coping Mechanisms for Turbulent Times. . . 101
Reframing Negative Narratives. 102
Finding Solace in Supportive Communities . 104
Celebrating Emotional Milestones. 105

Chapter 12 Strategies for Self-Empowerment . . . 107
Affirmations and Visualization Techniques . . 107
Setting and Enforcing Healthy Boundaries. . 108

Continuous Learning and Growth. 111
Celebrating Personal Power 112

**Chapter 13 Embracing Grief, Loss, and
Serendipity** 115
Navigating Grief and Loss. 115
Finding Meaning in the Darkness 116
Lessons for the Journey Ahead. 117
Moments of Serendipity 118
A Universal Truth. 120

Chapter 14 Nurturing Spiritual Growth 121
Daily Spiritual Practices for Well-being . . . 121
The Joy of Spiritual Retreats. 123
Deepening Connections with the Divine . . 124
Sharing Spiritual Gifts and Insights 125

Chapter 15 Ascending to New Heights 127
Recognizing Life's Cyclical Nature 127
Welcoming New Beginnings After Endings . 128
Paving the Path for Others 130
A Lifelong Commitment to the Climb 131

Chapter 16 Reflections and Revelations 133
My Reflections 133
Life's Hidden Lessons and Our Cheer Squad . . 134
A Message of Hope and Inspiration
for Fellow Travelers. 135
Bridges, Bonds, and the Beauty of the Now . . 136

Chapter 17 Charting a Clear Course to Success . . 139
        Understanding the Importance of Direction 139
        Defining Your Personal North Star 140
        Cultivating Strength through Direction 142
        The Role of Passion in Defining Direction . 143

Conclusion 145

BONUS: My 12-Step Path to Overcoming Setbacks and Bouncing Back Higher. 147

Afterword 161

Acknowledgments 163

About The Author 167

FOREWORD

In the beats of my music and the stories of my life, I've come across tales that stick with me, that feel like they're part of my own journey. But let me tell you, no story has hit home quite like *The Deliberate Climb*, written by my Aunt Naise.

Reading her story felt like opening a window into the heart and soul of someone who has faced life's toughest battles head-on and came out swinging. My Aunt Naise's journey, as detailed in this book, isn't just a story. It's a powerful illustration of what it means to be resilient in the face of adversity. The way she's laid out her experiences, with raw honesty and vulnerability, makes this book not only engaging and easy to read, but deeply moving.

From the moment I turned the first page, I was drawn into a narrative that felt as real and vivid as if I was walking alongside her, sharing in her struggles and victories. Her storytelling is real and unfiltered, exposing the lows and celebrating the highs in a manner that makes you feel deeply connected to her journey. It's this honesty that makes *The Deliberate Climb* stand out. You're not just reading a book; you're getting to know a person, understanding their battles, and, most importantly, witnessing the incredible strength it takes to keep moving forward.

Aunt Naise's insights into resilience, particularly her emphasis on pushing forward after a setback and staying focused, resonate on a personal level. It's this perseverance that's the heartbeat of the book. She doesn't just tell you to keep going; she shows you how, making her story a blueprint for anyone facing their own challenges. Her thought process, always practical and forward-thinking, offers a guide on how to tackle obstacles without losing sight of your goals.

One aspect of Aunt Naise's story that I found especially compelling is how she highlights the role of physical exercise in maintaining mental health. In today's fast-paced world, where mental health often takes a back seat, this focus is both refreshing and necessary. It's a reminder that taking care of our bodies is as important as taking care of our minds and that the two are fundamentally linked.

As I read through *The Deliberate Climb*, I couldn't help but feel inspired by Aunt Naise's journey. Her book serves as a powerful reminder that no matter the hurdles we face, we have within us the capacity to overcome them. It's a message of hope and strength that I believe is essential, especially in today's world, where so many of us are facing various obstacles and setbacks.

To anyone picking up this book, know that you're holding more than just pages filled with words. You're holding a story of triumph, a guide to resilience, and a companion for those moments when the climb seems too steep. Aunt Naise's journey is a tribute to the human spirit's unstoppable will to overcome and to emerge stronger on the other side of adversity.

As her nephew, someone who's seen her determination firsthand and has been inspired by her strength, I'm incredibly proud of Aunt Naise. Not just for writing this book, but for being a living example of everything it stands for.

I wish Aunt Naise all the best with the publication of this book. I have no doubt that her story will touch the hearts of many, offering them the strength to face their adversities and the courage to overcome any hurdle put in their path. Here's to the journey ahead and to the many lives this book will undoubtedly inspire and transform.

Thank you, Aunt Naise, for sharing your journey with us. And to you, the reader, may you find within these pages the inspiration to undertake your own deliberate climb, equipped with the knowledge that no matter how tough the journey, you possess the strength to make it through.

With love and respect,
Simi (hooliganhefs)

INTRODUCTION

> *"Life's most transformative moments often arrive disguised in adversity, urging us to embark on a journey of rediscovery, resilience, and rebirth."*
>
> — **Naise Silapa**

Life is a roller coaster, filled with both breathtaking highs and gut-wrenching lows. There are times when the very ground beneath us seems shaky, testing our spirit and resolve. Yet, it's in these moments, when faced with adversity, that we truly discover who we are and what we're capable of.

My transformation is carved out of challenges. As you delve deeper into these pages, you'll travel with me through life's storms and sunny spots, witnessing every stumble, setback, and surge forward.

Many of the events might seem eerily familiar—career twists, personal losses, broken dreams, and the looming cloud of uncertainty. But here's the thing: it's not about what happens to us, but how we respond, that truly shapes our destiny. This narrative aims to showcase the transformative magic of taking purposeful steps, even when the path seems unclear.

Attitude of mind matters. Rather than looking for signs of impending doom, look at life's hurdles as challenges, powerful agents of change. Facing adversity can unveil our hidden strengths and ignite a fire within, driving us to keep pushing, no matter what happens. Every purposeful step we take is a step towards a better version of ourselves.

The Deliberate Climb isn't just my story; it's a beacon for anyone feeling lost amidst life's tempests. With each page, you'll uncover insights, tactics, and genuine wisdom drawn from my personal journey, lighting the way from struggles to success.

More than anything, this book stands as a tribute to our incredible ability to bounce back. It showcases how we can transform setbacks into stepping stones, and doubts into dreams. As you join me on this climb, remember that no mountain is too high and no challenge is too great. Success is always within reach if we're determined.

I hope this book inspires, enlightens, and empowers you as you kickstart your own ascent from trials to triumphs. Embrace every challenge, celebrate every win, and let the art of deliberate action elevate you.

So, let's go on this climb together, side by side, scaling this mountain of hope and grit, remembering that beyond every stormy night, there awaits a brand-new dawn.

CHAPTER 1

THE FALL

*"Our greatest glory is not in never falling,
but in rising every time we fall."*

— Confucius

The Inception of the Climb

As I pen down the story of my deliberate climb, there's an image that vividly stands out in my memory—the moment I stood at the base of the Q1 Tower on Australia's Gold Coast. This towering structure, once the world's tallest residential building, presented a challenge that was more than just a physical ascent; it was a metaphorical representation of my life's journey.

The climb up the Q1 Tower wasn't just about conquering heights or testing my physical limits. It was a profound encounter with my deepest fears and a testament to the power of deliberate action. Each step upwards was a step out of my comfort zone, a direct confrontation with the anxieties and uncertainties that had long been my companions.

In many ways, this climb was a reflection of my life's path. Just like the uncertain steps I took up the tower, my journey through life has been a series of deliberate choices in the face of daunting challenges. From the serene landscapes of Samoa to the bustling streets of Australia, from the heartbreaking loss of loved ones to the betrayal of trust through an online scam, every hurdle was akin to a step on that tower.

But why start our journey together with this image of a climb? Because it perfectly encapsulates the essence of what I want to share with you. This book is not just about my story; it's about the universal journey of facing fears, overcoming obstacles, and the relentless pursuit of our goals—a journey I call "The Deliberate Climb."

So, as we embark on this narrative together, keep in mind the image of the Q1 Tower. It's a symbol of what we can achieve when we set our minds to it, a reminder that the view from the top can only be appreciated fully after the arduous ascent. It represents every daunting step I took, not just on that day, but throughout my life, and the transformative power of facing challenges head-on.

My Story

Our life on the small hobby farm, outwardly picturesque, was in reality far from perfect. The children seemed content, yet beneath the surface, I was battling a storm of emotions. Juggling the roles of a mother, wife, provider, and stepmother was a mountainous challenge.

The creek on our property was more than just a part of the landscape; it was my refuge, a place where I could be unreservedly myself. Hidden away from the bustle of the house, it was here that I allowed myself to be vulnerable. In this sanctuary, I could shed tears, seek Divine guidance, and muster the strength to keep going. My days were a relentless cycle of working full-time, studying, being a mother, and pursuing side hustles, all in a quest for a semblance of freedom that seemed just out of reach. But these endeavors, instead of liberating me, ensnared me deeper into an invisible pit of exhaustion and unspoken despair. The accusations of selfishness stung deeply, considering that my every waking moment was dedicated to building a better future for my family. I felt depleted, unappreciated, and overburdened, yet driven by the need to provide for my three children and to ease the burden that weighed heavily on me.

My mother, always a pillar of support, offered advice, but I felt trapped in a hole of my own making. It felt as if finding a solution to my problem was up to me. The pivotal night was when my husband announced his desire for freedom. He wanted to end our relationship. It was more than just a shock; it felt like a betrayal of all the years I had invested. Each day of toil, every tear shed in the hope of a better future for us as a family, now seemed in vain. My heart not only skipped beats in shock, but also ached with the realization that my sacrifices and efforts were unrecognized, unappreciated. The life I had painstakingly built with sweat, tears, and hope was unraveling before my eyes. My world came to a standstill. The revelation that our shared life of two decades was abruptly ending left me gasping for breath, a mix of disbelief and piercing heartache engulfing me. As I braced for the new chapter that lay ahead, practicalities took over. In preparation for our changed circumstances, we organized skip bins, booked trucks, and our families came to help us move.

Our lives were set for a significant transition following the sale of our farm. In the midst of this upheaval, my husband, who had yet to find a place of his own, moved in with us temporarily. This arrangement was meant to ensure the children's smooth transition into our new home. Despite the emotional complexity, I agreed, prioritizing their well-being.

The day arrived when it was time for my husband to finally leave. It was a moment fraught with mixed emotions. Standing at the threshold of our new home, I felt a chapter closing as I handed him our wedding rings—a symbolic end to our shared journey. Our children, witnessing this final farewell, were overcome with grief. Their father's departure marked the reality of our new life. Watching them cry broke my heart more profoundly than the end of our marriage itself. Their tears spoke volumes of their inner turmoil and shattered innocence.

In that moment, I realized the immense resilience required not just for me but for our children, too. It was a poignant reminder of how life's changes impact us all, especially the young hearts that rely on us for stability and love.

I juggled the remnants of our past, both financially and emotionally, seeking to rebuild and heal. Following these events, I faced financial and emotional turmoil. I filed for bankruptcy and started therapy, seeking answers to profound questions: Why do I feel unloved? Where does my sense of self-worth lie? Who am I amidst these life changes? These questions, and many more, lingered unanswered as I struggled to find meaning and direction.

As time passed, life with the kids began to feel more stable. Consulting a church dating site, as suggested by a friend, marked the beginning of a new phase of self-discovery. Little did I know, this step would lead me down a path of significant transformation and challenges. It tested me in ways I never imagined.

Once again, my world had been shattered. The catalyst for this upheaval was an encounter on the online dating site, where I met an individual claiming to be a single professional who had lost his wife to cancer. He said he was seeking a partner. Intrigued by the prospect of finding what I believed at the time would be fulfillment for me, I decided to explore this connection.

This person artfully employed psychological techniques, skillfully gaining my trust by purposely mirroring my thoughts and emotions. Over a period of four months, our conversations grew more personal, my guard was lowered, and I unknowingly followed the path he laid out for me.

His deception knew no bounds as he crafted a compelling narrative about securing a lucrative contract to oversee the construction of a dam in Africa. Urgently needing funds to finance the project, he sought assistance, tugging at my heartstrings with tales of personal tragedy and desperate circumstances. My trust in him grew, fueled by flattering words and constant reassurances that he cared deeply for me.

Despite my instincts raising alarms, I found myself ensnared by a web of deceit. I was manipulated into providing financial aid and rationalizing each demand for funds.

As months passed, the requests for money escalated, painting a picture of misfortune and mounting financial pressures. Unable to resist his pleas, I exhausted all avenues to secure funds, even resorting to borrowing money, lying to friends and family. The fear of losing what I had invested in this relationship was too powerful to escape.

One weekend, I visited my mother, clinging to hope that he would be the one for me, even though I hadn't heard from him in days. Every time I tried to picture him safely returning to the U.S., my mind spiraled into dark alleys of fear. Doubt, worry, and trepidation clouded my thoughts, pushing me into survival mode. My heart and mind clashed, torn between logic and emotion, between hope and despair.

But as the saga unfolded, I began to sense that something was amiss. A nagging doubt gnawed at my conscience, and I dared to question the validity of the situation. Regrettably, it was too late—I had already been manipulated and drained of my hard-earned savings.

In the wee hours, as the clock showed 3 a.m., a message flashed on my phone. Hope surged, but it was quickly extinguished. The final blow came when I believed he was finally coming home, only to discover that he had vanished, leaving me with a shattered heart, depleted savings, a mountain of debts, and a sense of worthlessness. There it was—another request for money, more emotional manipulation. A profound realization dawned on me: I had been played. I had fallen victim to a professional scam, a painful truth that left me feeling defeated and betrayed.

As disappointment coursed through me, I whispered a prayer, seeking forgiveness for my blindness. I was drained—emotionally, physically, and financially. Yet, in the silence of that night, as more messages lit up my screen, I found peace. I basked in the newfound emptiness, free from blame or tension. With a light heart, I fell into a deep sleep.

The morning sun warmed my face as my mother gently woke me. She sensed my turmoil, her concerned gaze probing for answers. I put on a brave face, avoiding her questions, and I focused on breakfast and the road ahead.

Tears blurred my vision as I drove away from my mother's house. The weight of everything that had transpired pressed on me. I pulled over, raising my eyes to the heavens, and found myself praying. I acknowledged my weaknesses, the emotional scars, and my inability to navigate this storm alone. It was a heartfelt cry to a power greater than me. With each tear shed, the weight lifted a little, making room for hope and healing.

The rest of the drive home was a journey of self-awareness. I immersed myself in the present, feeling the warmth of the sun, the comfort of the seat, and the taste of apple juice on my lips. Each moment became a tether, grounding me. I didn't resent the scammer; instead, I forgave him. Understanding, even just a little, why he might have done it brought relief. This forgiveness came from trying to understand his situation. Maybe he was desperate, needing the money more than me, or his family was in trouble. Recognizing that people worldwide face tough challenges and might act out of necessity, I found peace in forgiving him, seeing it as an act of empathy for his struggles.

There was no need to fight my emotions any longer or be resentful over lost money or mounting debts. I allowed myself to feel the pain, but with the knowledge that peace was within reach. I embraced the truth of my situation, seeking solace in the present moment and the Divine.

Admitting defeat is akin to swallowing a bitter pill. Sometimes, you might feel prepared for it externally, but internally, you're never truly ready. The weight of such an act in a world where I believed I had grasped the rhythm of life's dance; I was meticulously charting out each step. The stage was set, the plan laid out before me, and my intentions were clear. But as with any grand performance, an unexpected twist was waiting in the wings.

In the aftermath of the harrowing scam, I was determined to rebuild and reclaim control of my life. Yet, the Universe had other plans, hinting that my journey towards healing was going to be paved with unexpected lessons. With the scars of the past fresh and painful, I clung to familiar beliefs and habits. My internal resistance was palpable. I believed, rather stubbornly, that I could handle everything on my own, that seeking help was a sign of weakness, a fallacy crafted by past beliefs.

I was entrenched in a mental maze of my own making. There was an insistence to do everything alone, a stubborn refusal to acknowledge the need for external support. In reality, I was running away, letting my old paradigms dictate my life. A clear-thinking mind eluded me as my choices were clouded by the trauma of the scam.

But just as life has a way of knocking us down, it also has an uncanny ability to send reminders—wake-up calls, if you will. The Universe, in its infinite wisdom, orchestrated a dramatic and Divine intervention. In an unthinkable twist of fate, I was involved in a car crash, colliding head-on with a vehicle driven by a nun, of all people. The irony was not lost on me: she was on her way to a funeral. Both our vehicles bore the brunt of the collision, but miraculously, we emerged unscathed.

The initial shock made me believe I had grievously hurt, if not killed, a nun. The scene that followed was overwhelming. Sirens, flashing lights, and concerned faces from every direction converged on the accident site. Amidst the chaos, a surreal moment unfolded when men attempting to assist the nun discovered her immersed in prayer inside the car.

With a serenity that seemed otherworldly in that frantic scenario, the nun reached out, held my hand, and offered prayers not just for herself but for me. Her touch on my hand transcended the physical; it was a balm for the soul. There I was, trembling, almost drowning in guilt and shock, and yet, in this bewildering situation, a guiding light shone through.

It was a watershed moment. A realization dawned on me: I had been so caught up in the shadows of my past that I had failed to live in the present. My actions and decisions, driven by unresolved emotions and traumas, were pulling me back. If I were to truly move forward, I needed to be more intentional in my choices. Embracing the present and letting go of past hurts were the only ways to craft a brighter future.

The accident served as a poignant reminder that healing is a journey, not a destination. I hadn't given myself the necessary time and space to truly heal from the scam ordeal. My subconscious was still trapped in those dark days, impacting my decisions and reactions.

Here are my lessons learned: **Seeking help is strength, not weakness.** It's okay to lean on others. Sometimes, it's the external perspectives and support that give us the strength to march on.

The Power of the Present: Dwelling on past misfortunes hampers our ability to enjoy and appreciate the present. Letting go is not just about moving on; it's about making space for new experiences and joys.

Healing Is Personal: Everyone's journey to recovery is unique. It's crucial to give ourselves the time and patience to heal, physically and mentally.

Life's unpredictable nature means we're constantly learning, growing, and evolving. Every stumble and every setback is an opportunity to rise higher, embrace change, and come back stronger. As I continue on my journey, I'm grateful for every lesson—they've molded me, shaped my resilience, and made me who I am today.

In the aftermath of this devastating experience, I found myself facing a mountain of debt and an overwhelming sense of despair. But in the depths of my pain, a moment of clarity emerged—a "never again" moment that would alter the course of my life forever.

In that transformative moment, I decided to take accountability for my circumstances, understanding that if change were to come, it was up to me. I embraced the belief that the me I envisioned was the me I would become.

With newfound determination, I embarked on a journey of self-discovery and empowerment. I acknowledged that the pain I endured was temporary and the reward for my efforts would be immeasurable. My journey to rebuild my life had begun.

Through sacrifice, courage, determination, and discipline, I made a solemn commitment to repay my debts and reclaim my life. One step at a time, I confronted my financial obligations, working tirelessly to settle every penny I owed.

Days turned into months and months into years, but I persevered with unwavering faith in my ability to rise above the challenges. And so, in a remarkable span of just thirty months, I triumphed over adversity, paying off personal debts amounting to $198,000 as a single mother, saving for a deposit to begin my property investing journey, starting a business, and writing a book.

The transformation was profound, not just financially, but within my very being. As I stood atop the mountain of my accomplishments, I realized that the journey had not only taught me about resilience and perseverance but had also illuminated the strength within me to search and go deeper to find my true self.

Today, I stand with my head held high, having rebuilt my life and my sense of self-worth. The scars of the past are reminders of the battles I fought and won. I have learned to trust my instincts, to be cautious but not afraid, to recognize my own completeness, and to discern between genuine connections and deception.

I share my story not as a tale of woe but as evidence to the resilience of the human spirit. It is a story of redemption and empowerment, a beacon of hope for anyone facing their own uphill climb. My journey has taught me that it is never too late to start anew, to pick up the pieces, and to emerge stronger than ever before.

As I continue to build a brighter future, I carry with me the invaluable lesson that no one is immune to deception, but with knowledge, vigilance, and the power of self-belief, we can conquer any mountain that stands in our way.

The Day Everything Changed

We all have them—days that start off ordinary but end up redefining our existence. These aren't mere calendar dates but moments that split our life into 'before' and 'after.' And on that day, everything changed for me. I woke up with no inkling of the storm that was to come.

As if by clockwork, the sun rose, the alarm chimed, and a new day beckoned. With a stretch and a yawn, life's familiar rhythm seemed in place. But life, as it often does, had a twist in store. Little did I know that this day would challenge everything I believed in and stood for. It would question my identity, my strength, my purpose, and my beliefs.

The contours of the day's events etched themselves indelibly in my memory. Every detail, no matter how insignificant it seemed at the time, took on new importance. The weather, the faces I encountered, the words exchanged, the emotions felt—all painted a vivid picture of an experience that became a fulcrum of change.

As hours unfurled, the unexpected events that transpired felt like a cruel joke by the Universe. Suddenly, the world I knew crumbled, and the rug of stability was yanked from beneath my feet. The sensation was like free-falling, with no parachute to break the fall. The stomach-churning realization that life would never be the same again was paralyzing.

In the aftermath, a gamut of emotions took hold. Shock, denial, anger, sadness, confusion. Why me? Why now? The questions were incessant, with answers evasive. Every comfort zone I had built, every expectation I held, every dream I harbored seemed to be laughingly dismissed by fate. The safety net I had meticulously woven had gaping holes.

Yet, amidst the chaos, something crucial happened. The seeds of transformation were inadvertently sown. Though I didn't realize it at the time, this day of reckoning was setting the stage for a profound metamorphosis. It was a wake-up call, shaking me from complacency, pushing me into a crucible of growth, and prompting a journey of introspection and resurgence.

In the vast digital realm, the internet shines brightly as a beacon of knowledge, opportunities, and connections. Yet, as with any powerful invention, it has its dark corners, filled with illusions and traps. I, unfortunately, ventured into one of these shadowed nooks, getting caught in an online scam.

It started simply enough—an enticing email, a click, and a captivating website. The promise of the digital age is seductive: instant solutions, transformative opportunities, and the allure of shortcuts. During a moment of hope and vulnerability, I was ensnared.

This scam wasn't just about monetary loss, which was significant. It was also a blow to my trust and self-esteem. Questions arose: How did I fall for this? Why didn't I see the red flags? Every new email and online interaction became a source of anxiety. My safe digital haven had turned into a minefield of doubt.

For a while, I wallowed in self-blame. I felt embarrassed, replaying my actions, and thinking about what I could've done differently. But as the initial shock subsided, clarity emerged. This harsh experience, while devastating, was also deeply educational.

It made me more discerning, more cautious online. I realized the importance of listening to my gut feelings, of double-checking before making any decisions.

This episode also underscored the double-edged sword that is the internet. While it's an avenue of immense possibilities, it's also fraught with pitfalls. To truly reap its benefits, we must tread with a balance of hope and caution.

As the days turned into weeks and months, my perspective began to shift. Those digital scars? They transformed into reminders of resilience, of the ability to bounce back and grow from adversity. This wasn't just a tale of digital deceit—it became a testimony to the human spirit's strength and adaptability.

Our digital age, with all its convenience, also brings unique challenges. Scams and deceptions might be just a click away, but so are lessons in resilience and growth. This isn't a story of mere victimhood but a celebration of human resilience. Like many, I've been tested by life's illusions, but it's our response to these challenges that truly defines us.

More significantly, this confrontation with digital deception highlighted the dual nature of the digital age. While it holds immense potential, it's also rife with pitfalls. And navigating this terrain requires both enthusiasm and caution, hope and skepticism.

One of the most profound realizations from this experience was understanding the interconnectedness of our virtual and real lives. In a world where we often draw lines between our online personas and our offline selves, this incident was a stark reminder that our digital actions have real-life consequences.

The pain of a digital betrayal isn't confined to the pixels on a screen—it pierces the heart and shakes the soul.

Furthermore, it emphasizes the role of community and support systems in healing. No one is truly insulated from the potential pitfalls of the digital age. However, it's through collective wisdom, shared experiences, and mutual support that we can guide each other towards safer, more fulfilling online interactions. By openly discussing our digital missteps, we not only heal ourselves but potentially prevent others from facing similar fates.

And, while the internet is vast and seemingly infinite, it's essential to remember our intrinsic human values. Compassion, understanding, and genuine connection can't be replaced or replicated by any algorithm. As we navigate the digital world, let us carry these values with us, making the internet a more understanding and empathetic space for all.

In the end, the scars of this digital betrayal became badges of honor. They stood as an illustration of my ability to rise from setbacks, to learn from mistakes, and to transform pain into power. They reminded me that while the virtual world has its deceptions, the real world holds the keys to genuine growth, recovery, and resilience.

In the vast landscape of the digital age, deception often lurks in the most unexpected corners. In essence, this journey through the digital maze isn't about the perils of the internet alone. It's a broader reflection on life's unpredictable challenges and the incredible human capacity to rise above them. Through understanding, introspection, and steadfast determination, we can not only confront but also conquer any adversity thrown our way. Life might be filled with unexpected twists and turns, but armed with wisdom and experience, we can navigate it with confidence and grace.

The First Step to Rising

Acceptance isn't just about reconciling with our past; it's about anchoring ourselves in the present and keeping our gaze fixed on the future. It's about realizing that in this very moment, despite past setbacks, we hold the power to shape our destiny.

In the wake of my ordeal, I faced a profound truth: Life won't always go as planned. There will be storms that we never saw coming. We may not control the winds that disrupt our sails, but we can adjust our sails to ride the winds. And that control starts with acceptance.

Many people, when struck with adversity, fall into the dangerous trap of comparison. "Why did this happen to me when everyone else seems to be cruising smoothly?" But life isn't a competition of experiences. Every individual's journey is unique, filled with its own set of challenges and triumphs. Rather than measuring our challenges against someone else's, acceptance teaches us to focus on our own path, understanding that everyone has their battles, visible or not.

Acceptance, a term often thrown around so lightly, weighed heavily on me during my darkest days. When life seemed to unravel before my very eyes, the idea of simply "accepting" the cascading changes felt both alien and insurmountable. Every waking moment was a cocktail of stress, fear, and anxiety, with the lingering question: How do I truly accept this?

Battling these tumultuous emotions wasn't an overnight endeavor. It required a deliberate and conscious effort to bring order amidst the internal chaos. The turning point for me was understanding a simple yet profound truth: While I couldn't alter the past, I had the power to shape my reaction to it.

Acceptance is not about being passive; it's about empowering oneself. One of the first steps I took was grounding myself in the present. Often, our fears stem from either dwelling on past mistakes or fearing future consequences. By being present, we can tackle challenges as they come rather than being paralyzed by the "what-ifs."

Another valuable tool I discovered was open communication. Sharing my fears and anxieties with trusted loved ones provided a fresh perspective and often highlighted that many of my concerns were magnified in my mind. Sometimes, merely voicing our fears diminishes their power over us.

Additionally, I took to journaling as a means of self-reflection. Writing down my feelings, fears, and hopes allowed me to process and analyze them objectively. Over time, I could see patterns, recognize triggers, and equip myself better for future challenges.

Lastly, embracing a daily mindfulness or meditation practice can be transformative. Even just a few minutes a day can provide a mental sanctuary, allowing us space to breathe, reflect, and find clarity.

In the end, acceptance was not a destination but an ongoing journey. Every challenge, every fear, every setback became a stepping stone toward deeper understanding and inner peace.

By focusing on the present, seeking support, and equipping oneself with tools to navigate the mental maze, acceptance becomes not just feasible but empowering. Through this journey, I learned that while we might not always control the external world, our internal world is ours to shape, mold, and direct towards a path of resilience and hope.

Gradually, amidst the emotional whirlwind, a realization began to crystallize. The past, no matter how cherished or desired, was unchangeable. The only malleable, actionable moment was the present. And while the pain was real, continual resistance to the new reality only compounded the agony.

Additionally, acceptance is a gateway to self-compassion. In moments of despair, we're often our harshest critics. "I should've seen it coming." "I could've done better." But what if, instead of being our own worst enemy, we became our biggest supporter? Acceptance allows us to replace self-criticism with self-compassion. By treating ourselves with the same kindness and understanding that we'd offer a friend, we open the doors to healing and growth.

It's also important to note that acceptance doesn't equate to complacency. It's not about saying, "This is my lot in life, and there's nothing more to be done." On the contrary, acceptance is about recognizing and coming to terms with our current reality, which then empowers us to move forward with clarity and purpose. It gives us the courage to say, "This happened, but what's my next step?"

Interestingly, the beauty of acceptance often lies in the community it brings forth. When we're open about our struggles and the path to acceptance, it creates a ripple effect. Sharing our journey encourages others to share theirs, creating a web of interconnected stories, all rooted in the strength of the human spirit. It fosters a sense of belonging and reminds us that we're never truly alone in our struggles.

Lastly, acceptance gifts us the lens of gratitude. When we stop resisting our current reality and start embracing it, we notice the silver linings. The friends and family who stand by our side, the lessons we glean from adversity, the strength we didn't know we had—these become our focal points. And in doing so, we start to understand that every experience, good or bad, contributes to the rich tapestry of our lives.

In conclusion, acceptance isn't merely a passive acknowledgment of our circumstances. It's a dynamic, empowering force that propels us forward. It reminds us that while we cannot change the past, we have the agency to influence our future. By embracing the lessons of yesteryears and the potential of tomorrow, we march ahead, undeterred, crafting a narrative of hope, fortitude, and unyielding spirit.

The Genesis of Proactive Transformation

In life's chessboard, one can choose to be a pawn or a player. The difference lies in proactivity. When adversity struck, my initial reaction, like that of many, was one of reactivity. The shock, the pain, and the sense of betrayal left me in a reactive state, constantly on the defense, perpetually in a mode of damage control. But as days turned into weeks and weeks into months, I realized that to truly overcome and rebuild, I had to switch gears.

Being proactive meant more than just taking charge. It meant envisioning a brighter future despite the present gloom. It meant creating strategies instead of just coping. It meant taking calculated risks, making informed decisions, and, most importantly, believing in the possibility of a better tomorrow.

The shift to a proactive approach required both mental and practical changes. Mentally, it involved changing my internal narrative. Instead of seeing myself as a victim of circumstances, I began to view myself as a survivor, a warrior equipped with experience, wisdom, and resilience. This change in self-perception ignited the spark of self-belief, a crucial element in proactive living.

On a practical level, being proactive meant setting clear goals and charting a road map to achieve them. I began to educate myself, seeking knowledge, tools, and resources that would aid my journey. From financial literacy to emotional well-being, I dove deep, arming myself with the skills required to navigate the complexities of my new reality.

A proactive approach also meant seeking and building a supportive network. No man is an island, and in times of crisis, a supportive community can make all the difference. By reaching out, sharing my story, and connecting with others, I not only found support but also opportunities to give back to guide others in their journeys, reinforcing my belief in collective growth.

With time, the benefits of this proactive approach became evident. Life's challenges, though still present, seemed less daunting. Each obstacle became an opportunity to learn, adapt, and evolve. The sense of control that being proactive provided was empowering. It reminded me that while I couldn't change the past, I had the agency to shape the future.

In essence, while the fall was unexpected and painful, it set the stage for a deliberate climb. A climb powered by acceptance and proactivity, two potent forces that transformed adversity into an adventure, a journey of rediscovery, resilience, and revival.

CHAPTER 2

SPIRITUAL FOUNDATIONS

"Faith does not eliminate questions. But faith knows where to take them."

— Elisabeth Elliot

A Return to Inner Peace

Inner peace is a sanctuary, a serene oasis amidst the chaos of external life. It's not just the absence of turmoil but the presence of equilibrium, the harmonious coexistence of thoughts, emotions, and spirit.

Life has an uncanny way of reminding us of our inherent strength, often in moments when we feel most vulnerable. The adversity I faced wasn't just a series of unfortunate events; it was a litmus test of my inner resolve.

The immediate aftermath of a setback is clouded with doubt. We question our capabilities and, often, our self-worth. But as the dust settles and the rawness of the pain begins to fade, what emerges is a clearer understanding of our internal reservoir of strength.

In the wake of adversity, this inner peace often becomes elusive. The storms of doubt, regret, and fear threaten to drown the gentle whispers of tranquility. Yet, it's precisely in these tumultuous moments that a return to inner peace becomes paramount.

The journey back to this sanctum of serenity began with the understanding that inner peace is an innate state of being, not a destination to reach. Much like the calm depths of an ocean remain undisturbed despite the raging waves on its surface, our core remains tranquil amidst life's upheavals.

Through my trials, I learned that strength isn't just about physical endurance or mental stamina. It's about emotional resilience, the ability to pick up the shattered pieces of one's heart and begin the painstaking process of rebuilding. It's about spiritual fortitude, the unwavering faith that even in the darkest hours, there's a glimmer of light guiding us forward.

To reconnect with this peace, the first step was mindfulness. By grounding myself in the present moment, by anchoring my awareness to the here and now, I began to transcend the incessant chatter of the mind. Activities like meditation, deep breathing, and even simple walks in nature became gateways to this mindfulness, offering glimpses of the serene oasis within.

But a sustained return to inner peace required more than just mindfulness; it necessitated self-compassion. The adversities I faced had sown seeds of self-doubt and self-criticism. By embracing self-compassion, I began to heal these internal wounds, to treat myself with the same kindness and understanding I'd offer a dear friend.

As days turned into weeks and weeks into months, this combination of mindfulness and self-compassion began to bear fruit. The turbulent waves of emotions started to ebb, revealing the tranquil depths beneath. The past's shadows began to recede, illuminated by the radiant glow of inner peace.

The journey to tapping into this strength involves introspection, reflection, and often, forgiveness—forgiveness towards oneself for past mistakes and perceived failures. It's a realization that our strength isn't determined by the absence of challenges but by our response to them.

In essence, the return to inner peace was a homecoming, a rediscovery of my spiritual essence. It reinforced the belief that no matter the external chaos, a sanctuary of serenity exists within each of us, waiting to be embraced and cherished.

Trusting God's Plan

Life's tapestry is vast, intricate, and often beyond the comprehension of our limited perspectives. Every thread, every weave, has its place, its purpose. While individual events might seem random or even painful, from a broader vantage point, they all fit perfectly, creating a masterpiece of experiences.

Trusting God's plan or, if you prefer, the Universe's plan, wasn't an immediate epiphany. The adversities I faced, at first glance, seemed like cruel twists of fate, inexplicable and unjust. But as time progressed and the lens of perspective widened, a profound realization dawned: every challenge, every setback, was a part of a grander design, a cosmic orchestration leading to growth, wisdom, and enlightenment.

To trust God's plan is to embrace the concept of Divine timing. It's to understand that while our desires might have a certain timeline, God operates on a different rhythm, ensuring that everything unfolds at the perfect moment for the highest good.

It also means recognizing the interconnectedness of all events. The setback I faced wasn't an isolated incident; it was a catalyst, propelling me towards self-discovery, bouncing back, and spiritual growth. It was a chapter in a larger narrative, a story where challenges are not obstacles but opportunities, guiding us towards our true purpose.

This trust in God's plan also brought with it a profound sense of surrender. Not a surrender of inaction or defeat, but a surrender of control, an acknowledgment that while we can steer the ship of our lives, the ocean's currents, guided by God or the Universe, will determine our path.

This surrender was liberating. It alleviated the burdens of anxiety, fear, and overthinking, replacing them with faith, hope, and a deep-seated belief in the benevolence of the Universe.

In conclusion, trusting God's plan or the Universe's plan, whatever higher power you believe in, is not just a spiritual concept; it's a transformative way of life. By relinquishing the illusion of control and embracing Divine timing, we align ourselves with cosmic rhythms, ensuring that even in the darkest nights, we are guided by the Universe's benevolent stars.

The Power of Surrender

Life has a peculiar way of teaching us the most profound lessons when we least expect it. Amidst the dark clouds of deceit, when the scam ordeal unfolded, a silver lining emerged in the form of surrender. It wasn't about admitting defeat; it was a transformative realization, a profound awakening to the potent power that lies in letting go. My story, as illustrated in the book, is a testament to how surrender can be the beacon that guides us out of the depths of crisis and onto a path of healing and triumph.

In our lives, we often equate control with power. We believe that by clutching tightly to our desires, aspirations, and dreams, we can steer our destiny. However, the scam ordeal, as agonizing as it was, challenged this belief. It stood as a stark reminder that no matter how firm our grip on life, certain situations will slip through our fingers like grains of sand. But here's where the magic happens: when our hands are no longer clenched, they're open—open to receive, to embrace, and to set a new direction.

Surrender, as I have beautifully demonstrated through my journey, isn't a sign of weakness. On the contrary, it is an act of courage. It requires immense strength to accept my vulnerabilities, to acknowledge my limitations, and yet decide to move forward. While the scam was a painful detour from the path I envisioned, the act of surrendering redirected me towards a path I needed, filled with healing, introspection, and rediscovery.

There's a transformative alchemy in surrender. It changed my trajectory. Instead of spiraling downwards into a whirlpool of despair, surrender acts as the force that propels us upwards. It's a pivot point, marking the end of what was and the beginning of what could be. In my case, this shift was evident. I transitioned from being a victim of a cruel deception to being the protagonist of my own triumphant narrative.

Surrender also paves the way for healing. It is akin to cleaning a wound, allowing it to breathe, and giving it the space to heal naturally. By accepting the realities of the scam, I allowed myself the grace to process the pain, the betrayal, and the loss. This acceptance acted as a salve, mending not just the external damages but also the deeper emotional and spiritual wounds. It was the first step in rebuilding, in regaining trust—not just in others, but more importantly, in myself.

Moreover, rising from a crisis requires a recalibration of our internal compass. When faced with adversities like the scam, it's easy to lose our bearings. Here, too, surrender plays a pivotal role. By letting go of the weight of anger, regret, and resentment, we become lighter, more agile, and more attuned to the positive energies around us. It becomes the process through which we filter out the noise and tune into our inner voice, guiding us towards our true north.

My story is an inspiration for all. It serves as a poignant reminder that even in our darkest hours, there lies an opportunity to find light. Surrender is not about giving in; it's about breaking free from the chains of our past and emerging stronger, wiser, and more resilient. As you journey with me through the pages of the book, you'll discover that surrender isn't the end; it's a beautiful beginning. It's the dawn after the darkest night, promising a day filled with hope, healing, and endless possibilities. My triumph is a testament to the fact that when we embrace surrender, we don't just survive; we thrive.

Lessons in Faith and Resilience

In the labyrinth of life, faith is our compass, and resilience is our strength. Together, they form an indomitable duo that can help us navigate the most tempestuous storms and reach the shores of hope.

Faith, in its essence, is the belief in the unseen. It's the conviction that even in the bleakest moments, a higher power is guiding us, ensuring our well-being and growth. After my trials, faith took on a renewed significance. It wasn't just a spiritual tenet but a lifeline, a beam illuminating the path ahead.

Faith taught me patience. It made me realize that healing and recovery are not instantaneous but processes that require time, love, and nurturing. It also fostered a sense of surrender, an understanding that while we play a vital role in shaping our destiny, there are forces beyond our comprehension guiding our journey.

Then there's resilience, the incredible ability of the human spirit to bounce back from setbacks, to rise from the ashes, renewed and reborn. Resilience is not about avoiding pain but about facing it head-on, acknowledging its presence, and then moving past it with grace and determination.

My journey was strewn with challenges, moments of despair where the weight of circumstances threatened to crush my spirit. But each time, resilience emerged as the hero, reminding me of my inherent strength, my capacity to overcome, adapt, and grow.

It's worth noting that resilience isn't innate but cultivated. Each challenge, each setback, is an opportunity to build this muscle of resilience, to fortify our spirit for future adversities. By embracing faith and nurturing resilience, we not only equip ourselves for life's uncertainties but also transform our relationship with them. Instead of viewing challenges as burdens, we begin to see them as blessings in disguise, tools of the Universe to sculpt our character and spirit.

In sum, lessons in faith and resilience are not just about surviving life's storms but about thriving amidst them. They remind us that we are not mere passive recipients of fate but active co-creators of our destiny, capable of transforming challenges into foundations for a brighter, more enlightened future.

Embracing Spiritual Growth

There's an ancient adage that the lotus blooms most beautifully from the deepest and thickest mud. Similarly, our spiritual growth often finds its most potent catalyst in the crucible of adversity.

Adversity strips away the veneer of externalities, compelling us to delve deeper, to confront our true selves, to question our beliefs, values, and purpose. It acts as a mirror, reflecting not just our vulnerabilities but also our potential, our latent strength, and wisdom.

For me, the adversities I faced became profound spiritual teachers. They propelled me into a journey of self-discovery, introspection, and transformation. While the external world seemed chaotic, a silent revolution was brewing within, reshaping my spirit, refining my essence.

Adversity taught me gratitude. In moments of despair, I found solace in counting my blessings, cherishing the small joys, the fleeting moments of happiness and love. This focus on gratitude shifted my perspective from lack to abundance, from despair to hope.

It also deepened my connection with the Divine. Prayer, meditation, and spiritual readings became daily rituals, anchors grounding me in faith and hope. Through these practices, I began to sense a higher guidance, a benevolent force orchestrating events for my ultimate good.

Perhaps the most profound lesson adversity imparted was the impermanence of life. Everything, whether joy or sorrow, success or failure, is transient. This realization brought with it a profound liberation, freeing me from the chains of attachment, fear, and regret.

Embracing spiritual growth amidst adversity is a conscious choice. It's about seeking the silver lining in the darkest clouds, recognizing that challenges are not roadblocks but signposts guiding us towards a more enlightened, awakened existence.

In conclusion, adversity, while challenging, can be a potent catalyst for spiritual growth. By embracing the lessons it offers, by seeking its hidden blessings, we not only overcome its trials but also rise above them, emerging as more evolved, enlightened beings, attuned to the deeper rhythms of the Universe.

CHAPTER 3

EMBRACING THE LESSONS OF THE PAST

"Study the past if you would define the future."

— Confucius

Island Roots: Life in Samoa's Embrace

Amidst the vast Pacific Ocean lies the idyllic island of Samoa, my cherished homeland. Here, nestled amidst its natural beauty, my childhood was woven with stories of both joy and challenges.

In a typical Samoan setting, our home was a melting pot of generations. The air was filled with laughter, advice, and life's lessons as aunts, uncles, cousins, and my beloved grandma shared our living space. Our home was more than just a structure; it was a vibrant tapestry of shared lives, dreams, and histories.

However, when I was just nine, a tragedy cast a shadow over our sunny lives. My father's untimely demise in a plane crash was a shattering blow. His absence created a void, but our familial bond held us tight, offering solace. Recognizing the need for better opportunities for our family, my mother bravely ventured overseas two years later. In her absence, our home adjusted, with my grandma gracefully assuming the mantle of primary caregiver. My mother's sacrifice and her distant yet pivotal role were invaluable. With her being overseas, my grandma's wisdom and warmth played a crucial part in our upbringing, becoming our go-to for comfort and guidance.

Being one of the elder grandchildren, responsibilities came early. I was not just an older sibling but also a young caregiver, looking after my younger cousins. From the sizzle of cooking to the rhythm of daily chores, my days revolved around ensuring their well-being.

Yet, our home wasn't without its storms. Fridays, instead of heralding the promise of a weekend, brought with them trepidation. The predictability of an uncle's unruly behavior after a few drinks cast a dark cloud. The smallest provocations, like an undesired meal, would ignite his fury, leading to chaos. The consequences often spilled onto me, the protective elder one. We, the younger members, would often find solace in the hidden corners of our house or at an understanding neighbor's. A particularly painful memory involves a day at our family plantation, where a misplaced blow caused me to lose consciousness.

Outside home, challenges persisted. School days, which should've been about learning and friendships, had their moments of torment. I still recall the sting, both physical and emotional, when I struggled with English words, leading to ridicule and punishment. Fear became a constant companion, and with no one to confide in, I learned to mask my pain.

Such memories, though painful, have more to offer than mere scars. They can sometimes tether us to the past, impeding our growth and preventing us from evolving into our best selves. However, they also bring with them invaluable lessons about resilience, empathy, and the power of transformation.

With every challenge, there was also an intrinsic lesson. From the home's chaos, I learned the value of compassion and patience. From school's adversarial environment, the importance of perseverance and self-belief emerged. Today, as I reflect, I realize that it's essential to embrace these lessons, not just the memories, to forge ahead. For in our past lies the seed of our future growth.

Past as a Compass, not a Cage

It's said that those who do not learn from the past are doomed to repeat it. While the past can be a treasure trove of lessons, it can also become a prison, holding us captive with chains of regret and what-ifs.

For me, the past was initially a haunting specter, a constant reminder of all that went wrong. The mistakes made, the trust broken, the dreams shattered—each memory a sharp sting. As days passed, a change in perspective began to emerge.

Instead of viewing the past as a relentless jailer, I started to see it as a wise teacher. Each setback, each misstep, each heartbreak carried with it a lesson, a nugget of wisdom that, if heeded, could pave the way for a brighter future.

This transformational shift involved reframing my relationship with the past. It meant acknowledging the pain without letting it define me. It meant cherishing the good memories while learning from the painful ones. It meant realizing that while the past shapes us, it doesn't have to confine us.

By viewing the past as a compass, I was able to chart a course forward. I could avoid previous pitfalls, build on past successes, and forge a path that, while informed by history, was not restricted by it.

The Power of Reflection

In today's fast-paced world, pausing to reflect is often seen as a luxury. But reflection is not just a passive act of nostalgia; it's a potent tool for growth, understanding, and transformation.

The challenges I faced compelled me to retreat inwards to engage in deep reflection. This wasn't just about replaying events but about understanding them, seeking patterns, discerning lessons, and envisioning a different future.

Through reflection, I began to see the larger tapestry of life. I could connect the dots, seeing how events, people, and choices intertwined to shape my journey. I could appreciate the synchronicities, the seemingly random occurrences that, in hindsight, held profound meaning.

More importantly, reflection enabled emotional processing. By revisiting past emotions, I could understand, validate, and eventually release them. This emotional cleansing was cathartic, creating space for new experiences, feelings, and insights.

Adopting a regular practice of reflection, whether through journaling, meditation, or simple introspection, became a cornerstone of my healing journey. It provided clarity, fostered gratitude, and infused a deeper sense of purpose in my life.

Embracing the Wisdom of Experience

There's a silver lining to every cloud, a lesson in every trial, wisdom in every experience. While this may sound clichéd, it's a truth I came to embrace wholeheartedly.

The adversities I faced, while undoubtedly painful, were also profound teachers. They taught me about resilience, faith, patience, and the transformative power of hope. They made me realize the impermanence of material possessions and the enduring value of relationships, integrity, and inner peace.

With each challenge, I gained a deeper understanding of life's complexities and the nuanced interplay of fate and free will. I learned to appreciate the beauty in small moments, the joy of simple pleasures, and the invincible spirit of the human heart.

As I moved forward, this wisdom became a guiding light. Instead of lamenting lost opportunities, I celebrated gained insights. Instead of mourning what was, I cherished what had become. Embracing the wisdom of experience meant recognizing that life's greatest lessons often come disguised as challenges, and it's through navigating these challenges that we truly discover our essence.

Chapter 3 underscores the transformative power of the past. By reconnecting with our inner strength, viewing the past as a guiding compass, reflecting deeply, and embracing the wisdom of experience, we can turn past trials into stepping stones for a brighter, more enlightened future.

CHAPTER 4

LESSONS FROM BOB PROCTOR

"Thoughts become things. If you see it in your mind, you will hold it in your hand."

— Bob Proctor

The Genius Mind

Imagine climbing a mountain and suddenly seeing a guiding light: that's what Bob Proctor's wisdom did for me, especially his teachings about the incredible power of our minds.

Long before the sting of the scam touched my life, I found solace and guidance in Bob Proctor's teachings. Despite my previous studies in human behavior, I couldn't fathom how I had allowed my mind to be so easily swayed and manipulated during that fateful time. Yet, it was through Bob's enlightening materials that I discovered a source of reliance and clarity. He shed light not only on the intricacies of my actions but also on the fundamental reasons behind human tendencies and life's unpredictable events. This deeper understanding filled me with gratitude and revealed the dormant power within us all—a force that, when harnessed, can pivot any situation, no matter how bleak, towards a path of triumph.

Many people walk through life without realizing the mighty force they carry inside. They often think of their minds just as storage boxes for random thoughts and old memories. But diving into Proctor's teachings, I learned a game-changing truth: our mind isn't just a storage box; it's a powerhouse that can reshape our lives!

Think of the mind like a two-sided coin. On one side, if we let negative thoughts take over, it can hold us back like heavy chains keeping a bird from soaring. But flip that coin, and with the right understanding, our minds can lead us to achieve wonders. It's like the sun: on one hand, it can give us a sunburn, but when used rightly, it provides warmth and helps things grow.

Picture two people stuck on a deserted island. One person feels defeated, seeing no way out. The other, using his mind's power, finds endless possibilities, using what the island offers to not only stay alive but to flourish. This is the heart of Proctor's message: depending on *how* we use our minds, we can see challenges as dead ends or doors to amazing adventures!

Bob Proctor often talked about the intellectual faculties of the mind, describing them as our built-in superpowers. Imagine having a set of unique tools, each with a special ability, right inside your mind, waiting to be tapped into! From intuition, which gives us that gut feeling about something, to imagination, which lets us dream beyond the skies, these faculties offer limitless opportunities.

One of Proctor's most emphasized faculties is our will. Think of it as the captain of a ship, steering through stormy seas, deciding the course and direction regardless of the challenges. Our will, when strengthened, can help us stay firm on our path, no matter how many obstacles we face. It gives us the strength to say 'yes' to our dreams and 'no' to distractions.

Then there's our perception—the lens through which we see the world. It's like wearing glasses that can be adjusted. We can choose to see the world in grayscale, focusing on challenges and hurdles, or we can adjust our view, emphasizing the vibrant colors of opportunity and hope. By fine-tuning our perception, we have the power to transform our reality.

Memory is another magical faculty. While most of us use it to remember past events, Proctor encourages us to use it to envision our future. Imagine using your memory not just to recall the past but to pre-live the successes you aspire to achieve. It's like watching a movie trailer of your future successful self, making those dreams more tangible.

Proctor's teachings on the intellectual faculties remind us that our minds are not just reactive but proactive tools. We have the innate ability to shape our destiny, craft our reality, and turn our wildest dreams into achievable goals. Embracing the magic of our minds means unlocking doors we never even knew existed!

As I reflect on my own journey, I see the profound impact of these intellectual faculties in every twist and turn. In the darkest moments, when I felt ensnared by the financial scam and the weight of single motherhood, it was my intuition that whispered reassurances, telling me to persevere. My imagination, on the other hand, painted vivid images of a brighter future, inspiring me to forge ahead even when the path seemed bleak.

The power of my will became most evident as I tackled the mountains of debt. There were moments of fatigue, moments when giving up appeared as the easier route. But, just like a captain steering the ship steadfastly, my will kept me anchored to my mission. My perception, too, underwent a significant transformation. From initially seeing my challenges as insurmountable barriers, I gradually began recognizing them as stepping stones, each one elevating me closer to my dreams.

Lastly, as I embarked on this deliberate ascent, I started using my memory in the way Proctor described. Instead of just dwelling on past setbacks, I envisioned my future triumphs, feeling the joy and pride even before they materialized. This 'pre-living' powered my spirit, infusing my daily grind with purpose and passion. In essence, these intellectual faculties weren't just theoretical concepts from Proctor's teachings; they became the guiding stars, lighting up the path of my personal odyssey.

Creating a Personal Paradigm Shift

When I first stumbled upon the concept of paradigms, it was like someone had handed me a mirror. It reflected on parts of me that I hadn't realized were there. These paradigms, these old songs of doubt and fear, had quietly played in the background of my life for years, dictating my choices and coloring my world.

Each challenge I faced, from financial struggles, health scares, and a traumatic childhood to the roller coaster ride of single motherhood, felt like a mountain. But in reality, it wasn't just the external circumstances that made them daunting. It was those age-old beliefs, the whispering voices of doubt, that amplified each obstacle, turning molehills into mountains. The real struggle wasn't just what was happening around me but also within me.

Taking a cue from Proctor's teachings, I started viewing my life's challenges differently. Instead of letting those hidden paradigms control my story, I became the author. I chose which beliefs to keep and which ones needed rewriting. It wasn't an overnight process, but each day, I consciously chose hope over doubt, resilience over fear.

As I began this inner overhaul, the world around me started to shift. Just like a gardener who patiently tends to his garden, I began to see the fruits of my labor. The challenges didn't disappear, but they no longer felt insurmountable. With my new, empowered mindset, I faced them head-on, turning them into opportunities for growth.

In essence, my journey became a testament to the transformative power of changing one's inner dialogue. While external circumstances are often beyond our control, our reactions to them, shaped by our paradigms, are within our grasp. By shifting my inner narratives, I didn't just change my perspective; I transformed my entire world.

Setting Boundaries and Goals

This was another powerful lesson that also changed my life. Bob Proctor painted a clear picture: to achieve our dreams, we must first see them clearly and protect them fiercely. Just like a lighthouse guides a ship through dark waters, our well-defined dreams light up our path, ensuring we never lose our way, even when life throws curveballs at us.

During my roller coaster moments, I leaned into Proctor's wisdom about setting goals. I realized it wasn't just about knowing where I wanted to go; it was about passionately painting that picture in vibrant colors, making it so vivid that it became my North Star.

Think of it like this: imagine a ship sailing in vast open waters. Without a map or a specific destination, it'll float aimlessly, tossed about by every wave and whim. But, with a marked spot on the map, even turbulent waters can't deter its journey. That's what Proctor's teachings did for me—they gave me a map and a clear spot to sail towards.

But what about the challenges and naysayers we encounter? That's where boundaries come into play. Imagine them as the protective walls around a treasure chest, safeguarding the precious dreams inside. These walls ensure that no storm or invader can snatch away what we hold dear. They're our personal defense, keeping negativity and distractions at arm's length, ensuring our dreams remain undisturbed and pure.

In my own journey, these teachings weren't just theoretical concepts; they became my lifeline. I recall times when the weight of challenges threatened to snuff out my dreams. Financial hurdles, personal struggles, and the tireless role of being a single parent often left me feeling lost in life's vast ocean. But with every wave that tried to push me off course, my clearly defined goals acted as my anchor, grounding me and reminding me of the shores I was determined to reach.

Establishing boundaries, on the other hand, was akin to the crew and the safety measures on my ship. There were many external voices—skeptics, past failures, and societal norms, all trying to divert or discourage. Setting strong boundaries helped me filter out these distracting noises, ensuring that only voices of encouragement, hope, and belief echoed in my ears. Each time I fortified these boundaries, I learned an invaluable lesson: our dreams are sacred, and it's not only our right but our responsibility to protect them. Through my journey, illuminated by Proctor's wisdom, I discovered that with a clear vision and protective boundaries, no storm is insurmountable, and every dream is within reach.

Riding the Waves of Vibration

Have you ever thought about the energy that's buzzing all around us? Bob Proctor introduced this beautiful idea with the Law of Vibration. He believed that everything, from the biggest stars in the sky to our smallest dreams, hums with its own unique energy. And the energy we give off plays a huge part in what comes back to us, kind of like an echo in a vast canyon.

Think back to a time when everything seemed to be going wrong. For me, that was a period when I was surrounded by doubt and worry. It's like I was tuned into a gloomy radio station that only played sad songs. But Proctor gave me a fresh perspective. He said it's like having a radio dial—by filling our hearts with gratitude, love, and hope, we can turn that dial and tune into brighter, more cheerful stations.

Imagine having a radio that picks up different stations based on how you feel. Feeling down might get you a station playing gloomy tunes. But when you're happy and hopeful, it's all upbeat songs and positive vibes. That's how the Law of Vibration works! When I started to shift my focus and feel more positive, it's like the Universe took notice. Doors began to open, friendships grew stronger, and even the toughest times started feeling like building blocks to something bigger. I realized that by changing my inner tune, the Universe sang along with me, creating a melody of magic and miracles.

The Law of Vibration leads beautifully into another majestic concept: the Law of Attraction. It's like the Universe's way of saying, "Like attracts like." In other words, the energy we exude, whether positive or negative, draws experiences and situations of a similar nature. If we're broadcasting feelings of joy, love, and hope, the Universe seems to send more reasons for joy our way. On the flip side, if we dwell in negativity, we might find ourselves encountering more bumps on the road.

Looking back, there were phases where I felt trapped in a storm, every thunder echoing my inner turmoil. In those times, the Law of Attraction seemed to bring more clouds. But when I began to understand and harness this law, a profound shift occurred. I started focusing on my desires instead of my fears, on my dreams rather than my setbacks. The more I nourished my heart with hope and ambition, the more the Universe responded in kind. Roads that were once blocked miraculously cleared, and winds that were against me became supportive gusts pushing me forward. It was a revelation: the world around me was a mirror reflecting my inner state.

For anyone walking a path like mine, know this: your thoughts and feelings have power. They are like magnets, drawing experiences into your life. My story serves as a reminder of the magic that can unfold when we align our internal compass with our true north. So, take a moment each day to visualize your dreams, feel them deeply, and trust in the Universe's ability to bring them to fruition. By understanding the Law of Attraction, we learn that the pen to write our life's story truly rests in our hands.

Transforming Adversity into Achievement

Bob was always a beacon of wisdom, and when it came to the topic of perspective, his insights were unparalleled. His teachings often circled back to a singular idea: that our perspective, more than our circumstances, determines our reality.

One of Bob's favorite sayings was, "The storm doesn't shape us; our response to it does." Crisis, in Bob's eyes, was an external factor. But growth? That was all internal. He believed that our growth from crises wasn't defined by the crisis itself but by the lens through which we viewed it. Bob changed my life and helped me use my perspective to change how I saw anything in life that would help me move forward.

Think about a seed. Left on a table, it remains just that—a seed. But when buried, seemingly faced with a crisis, it begins to grow. In darkness, it finds its strength, shoots up, and blooms. According to Bob, we're not so different from seeds. When buried in problems, challenges, or crises, our true potential can sprout. But, for this to happen, perspective is key.

Bob often narrated tales from his own life during our trainings, drawing from the well of his experiences. A particularly poignant story was his business failure. To most, a business collapsing would mean the end. But not for Bob. He regarded it as a detour, not a dead end. He argued that while the facts of our situations, such as bankruptcy, a global pandemic, or a personal loss might be unchangeable, our narratives about them are entirely within our control. When his business crashed, instead of seeing them as failures, Bob viewed these incidents as a masterclass in entrepreneurship. He often said, "I didn't lose a business; I gained an MBA's worth of real-world experience."

This attitude was classic Bob. He didn't just preach perspective; he lived it. One of his notable teachings revolved around the concept of 'reframing.' Bob believed that the most challenging situations could be 'reframed' or viewed from a different angle. This reframing wasn't about sugarcoating reality or being overly optimistic, but about seeking out the growth potential in every situation. It was about asking, "What can I learn?" instead of "Why did this happen?"

Bob's reframing technique reminded everyone of the tale of David and Goliath. While everyone focused on Goliath's strength, David viewed the giant's size as his weakness. Bob reiterated that, like David, success in a crisis doesn't come from matching force with force but from shifting our perspective to uncover hidden advantages.

Bob often argued that growth was a choice. Crises were inevitable, but whether we grew from them was entirely up to us. He said that crises pushed us out of our comfort zones and, with the right perspective, into our growth zones. He often quipped, "Crisis introduces us to ourselves," emphasizing that the most challenging times often reveal strengths we never knew we had.

Toward the end of his teachings, Bob left everyone with a thought that cemented his philosophy. He said, "Our eyes show us what's there; our perspective shows us what's possible." In the vast canvas of life, where crisis and calm intermingle, Bob's teachings remind us that with the right perspective, we don't just weather the storm; we learn to dance in the rain.

In essence, Bob's teachings on perspective weren't just lessons—they were life strategies. Strategies that could turn the most significant crises into platforms for monumental growth and success. His teachings sure did help me shift my paradigms and way of thinking.

CHAPTER 5

MOTHER, THE GUIDING STAR

*"Life doesn't come with a manual,
it comes with a mother."*

— Unknown

The Foundations of Her Influence

Every powerful story has its roots, a foundation that shapes the entire narrative. For me, and for many others, this foundation was embodied by a mother. My mother was more than just the person who raised me; she was the epitome of steadfast strength and deep wisdom. Her life, marked by various challenges, became a collection of valuable lessons that I hold dear.

Imagine a resilient ship sailing through a fierce storm. Despite the raging waters trying to engulf it, the ship keeps moving forward with grace and determination. That ship is a metaphor for my mother. Her life wasn't a fairy tale with perfect endings. Rather, it was a story of overcoming tough challenges with bravery. She taught me, more through actions than words, that being resilient isn't just about surviving the tough times; it's about finding joy and serenity in them.

Her strength was accompanied by a grace that was almost otherworldly. In times of hardship, where others might falter, she remained strong, her wise insights shining brightly. She believed that true strength was not just about enduring difficulties but about firmly holding onto one's values and beliefs, even when things are uncertain. She taught me to find hope even in the darkest moments and to illuminate the way for others.

Her impact went beyond the stories she shared or the memories we made. It was something real and vibrant, a guide for living life with purpose, intention, and strong self-belief. As I faced my own life's challenges—from financial troubles to heartaches and times of self-doubt—it was her resilient spirit that resonated within me, guiding me and reinforcing my inner strength. She had this remarkable way of seeing the big picture, or what she called an "eternal perspective." Her life, with its ups and downs, served as a powerful reminder that we all have vast potential within us, waiting to be realized.

Maternal Memories-

Life is like a vast painting, each moment and memory adding its unique color and texture. Among these memories, the ones of my mother shine the brightest, like threads of gold weaving through the tapestry of my life.

Picture a young tree swaying in the wind, vulnerable, yet finding strength from its deep roots. These roots are like my mother's memories for me. They are the foundation of who I am. Memories of her comforting embrace, her empathetic tears reflecting my own pain, and her encouraging words are not just recollections. They are the pillars of my spirit, representing a love so deep and unwavering that no challenge could ever weaken it.

In a world where it's easy to be judged and hard to find kindness, my mother was my haven. She saw beyond my flaws and mistakes. She recognized the person I was beneath it all, someone still learning, growing, and sometimes stumbling. She believed in my potential, my future, and, most importantly, the goodness within me that I sometimes couldn't see.

Her saying, "No one can fix your life but you," has stayed with me. It might seem like a simple phrase, but its meaning is profound. Through these words, she taught me a powerful lesson. She constantly reinforced my inner strength, her faith in my ability to overcome obstacles, and her belief that, despite any setbacks, I had the capacity to stand up, transform, and start anew. This lesson has been my guiding star, leading me through life's challenges and reminding me of her wisdom at every turn.

Pearls of Wisdom

Every moment with my mother was like reading a new chapter from the book of life's lessons. She was more than a mother in the usual sense. To me, she was a wise mentor, a light guiding my way, and a trusted friend for sharing my deepest hopes and fears.

Among the many things she taught me, her belief in self-confidence stands out. I remember telling her about the scam that shattered my dreams. We sat together, and she looked at me with understanding. She reminded me that every downfall is a chance for a comeback. Even when I made big mistakes, she was always there, believing in me. Her saying, "Get back on the horse again," was her way of telling me I had the strength to rise from any setback.

During those trying times, I confided in my mother about a significant church calling I had received. Overwhelmed by the enormity of the role and my own personal turmoil following the scam ordeal, I was on the verge of declining. It was a period where my life felt upended, and the thought of dedicating myself to serving others seemed beyond my capabilities. Yet, it was my mother's profound insight and encouragement that shifted my perspective. "This is exactly what you need right now," she gently insisted, seeing beyond my immediate pain and turmoil. Her words were not just about urging me to accept the calling; they were about embracing a journey of healing and transformation.

She viewed this opportunity as a gateway to success, joy, fulfillment, and happiness despite the sorrow and trauma that clouded my vision. Her eternal perspective, always so keen and uplifting, reassured me that in serving others, I would not only help lift their spirits but would also find my own being uplifted. My mother believed that this act of service would catalyze a transformation within me, bringing about healing and positive change far quicker than I could have imagined.

Thus, inspired by her wisdom and driven by her belief in the healing power of helping others, I accepted the calling. It became a journey of not just fulfilling a calling but of rediscovering my own strength, joy, and purpose amidst adversity.

But the greatest lesson from her was about unconditional love. It's not the kind of love that changes with conditions; it's a love that sees through mistakes and remains strong through the toughest times. Through her support and actions, I learned to love unconditionally, to accept people for who they are, not for what they appear to be. This lesson transformed how I see the world, teaching me to meet people with compassion, understanding, and an open heart.

When I first shared the news of the scam with her, her reaction was full of empathy. She cried with me, feeling my pain. In her tears, I saw her unconditional love and understanding. There was no judgment from her, only pure love. Her belief in my ability to overcome and bounce back was unwavering. It felt as if she knew I would eventually recover, and it was only after I regained my footing that she peacefully transitioned to heaven. Her wisdom and love continue to guide me, shaping my path and my understanding of true love.

A Mother's Eternal Influence

As I climbed out of despair, heading towards hope and recovery, my journey took a significant turn. It was as if my mother, my guardian angel, was patiently waiting for me to find my footing and regain my strength before she peacefully moved on to her eternal life. The space she left in the physical world is vast, but the love and memories we shared still deeply resonate with me.

Our physical world is just a small piece of a much larger, more profound existence. There's a spiritual realm, unseen but always present, where our deepest connections, especially with our loved ones, continue beyond physical limits. Years have passed since my mother left this world, but her spirit, her essence, and her unconditional love still guide, nurture, and inspire me.

Every challenge I face, every success I achieve, feels like an echo of her enduring spirit and determination. The values she taught me, the principles she lived by, and the unwavering belief she had in me have become the foundation of all my dreams and achievements. It feels like with every milestone I reach, her pride and joy surround me, offering comfort and encouragement.

On days when life feels overwhelming, or I'm faced with uncertainty, I find solace in the memories we shared. I recall her laughter, her wise words, and the endless love she had for me. These precious memories are like a sanctuary, reviving my spirit and reigniting my drive to push forward. They remind me to see each challenge as a chance for growth, to transform adversities into opportunities, and to use my struggles as a force to drive me towards my goals.

My life's journey is more than a series of events; it's a continuous homage to her lifelong teachings, her steadfast beliefs, and her limitless love. In every decision I make and every path I choose, I feel guided by her. She was more than a figure from my past; she continues to be a guiding star, shining light on even the darkest paths of my journey, ensuring I find my way. As I walk through life, I deeply feel her absence, but it only makes me cherish her eternal presence in my heart even more.

The Anchor of Unwavering Belief-

In the turbulent seas of life, where adversity can toss us about, the unwavering belief of a loved one becomes our anchor, grounding us firmly amidst the chaos. It's this steadfast belief, often silent yet profoundly potent, that can illuminate our darkest hours and guide us through life's most challenging storms. The impact of having someone who believes in us unconditionally is immeasurable. It is a powerful force that not only holds us steady but also propels us forward, even when the odds seem insurmountable.

This enduring belief acts as a guiding light, helping us navigate the murky waters of doubt and fear. When someone believes in us without wavering, it instills a sense of hope and courage. It reinforces the notion that we are not alone in our journey, that our struggles are shared, and our triumphs are collectively celebrated. This kind of support transcends mere encouragement; it is a foundational pillar upon which we can rebuild and renew ourselves, no matter the extent of our tribulations.

For me, my mother's unwavering belief was a shining light during my darkest times. Her faith in me was not just comforting; it was transformative. It reminded me that belief is not just a sentiment; it's a catalyst for change. In moments of doubt, her conviction in my ability to overcome and thrive was the wind beneath my wings. It taught me that the strength to persevere and the resilience to bounce back are often fueled by the steadfast belief of those who care for us deeply.

This kind of unwavering belief is more than just confidence in someone's capabilities; it is a deep understanding of their potential, a recognition of their inherent worth, and an unshakable assurance in their ability to rise above challenges. It's a belief that doesn't waver in the face of setbacks but grows stronger, becoming a constant in an ever-changing landscape of life's trials and tribulations.

The importance of this belief cannot be overstated, especially during adversity. It becomes our emotional and spiritual anchor, offering stability when we are buffeted by life's unpredictable currents. It helps us maintain our course, even when visibility is low, and the destination seems far. The guidance and support from a loved one who believes in us unflinchingly can make all the difference in our journey. It can turn despair into hope, weakness into strength, and trials into triumphs.

In conclusion, the unwavering belief of a loved one is a priceless gift, a treasure that can change the course of our lives. It's a reminder that in the grand tapestry of existence, we are interconnected threads, each one's strength buoying the other. As we climb the mountains of our lives, let us cherish and celebrate these anchors of belief, for they are the silent heroes in our stories of resilience and redemption.

CHAPTER 6

NAVIGATING SINGLE MOTHERHOOD

"There is no force equal to a woman determined to rise."

— W. E. B. Du Bois

The Double Battle

The role of a mother is inherently multifaceted, but the challenges of single motherhood add another layer of complexity. As the main breadwinner, protector, and caregiver, a single mother's journey is laced with intricate webs of responsibilities and emotions. Yet, the unfaltering spirit of a single mother, epitomized by my own journey, showcases resilience in its truest form.

When I was faced with financial devastation, the battle wasn't just about personal healing. It was equally, if not more, about ensuring stability for my three children. While my inner world churned with anguish and confusion, the exterior was a bastion of strength and determination for them. The dichotomy was striking—inside was a soul grappling with betrayal and loss, while on the outside stood a mother, steadfast in her commitment to shield her children from life's cruelties.

Parenting is a daunting task. Every decision, every action, is intrinsically linked to the well-being of your children. But the role of a healing single mother meant shouldering two profound responsibilities. One was the onus of rebuilding a shattered financial foundation; the other was the more delicate task of nurturing young souls, ensuring they remained untouched by the storm that raged outside.

In every sleepless night and every arduous day, there was an unwavering resolve: not to let the scars of betrayal and adversity mar the innocence and joy of my children's world. They would wake up to the same loving face, the same warmth, and the same sense of normalcy, regardless of the tempests I faced.

In this journey, the silent strength of single motherhood emerged as an anthem of resilience. It reiterated that while wounds were many and challenges colossal, the spirit of a mother, determined to rise, would always overshadow them.

Celebrating Small Victories

Every ascent, no matter how steep, is marked by milestones—some monumental, others seemingly insignificant but equally pivotal. As a single mother wading through financial quicksand, I found solace in small yet profound victories.

Each day that passed without my children sensing the gravity of our situation was a victory. Each time their laughter echoed in our home, unaffected by the shadows of adversity, was a moment of triumph. It wasn't about monumental strides but the tiny steps that made life feel normal for them.

And then there were personal milestones. The first time I managed to save a small sum after the scam, the day I found the strength to venture out into the world and face people who might judge, the instances where I could rekindle my own sense of self-worth amidst the ruins—all of these were small yet immensely significant victories.

In the face of overwhelming odds, the tendency is often to wait for a grand turnaround, a sweeping moment of redemption. But life, especially the journey of a single mother, teaches you the invaluable lesson of celebrating the minuscule. It's in these tiny fragments of joy and achievement that one finds the energy to keep pushing forward.

Each small victory was a reminder that storms, no matter how fierce, are temporary. They served as bastions of hope, emphasizing that with determination and a never-give-up attitude, the dawn isn't too far.

These victories, both as a mother and as an individual, became the individual steps of my ascent. They were proof that even in the face of debilitating challenges, with unwavering resolve and the power of love, one can carve out moments of joy, achievement, and most importantly, hope.

Reinventing the Meaning of Success

In a world where success is so often quantified by materialistic metrics—the size of one's bank account, the brand of car one drives, or the exclusivity of one's address—the sting of financial betrayal could have easily trapped me in a quagmire of perceived failure. But as a single mother responsible for shaping the perspectives of three young minds, it became essential to redefine what success truly meant.

The initial days after the scam were tough. The whispering winds of society often carry tales of material successes, exacerbating the pain of financial loss. However, looking into the hopeful eyes of my children, I realized that I had an opportunity, a chance to impart a lesson far more valuable than any transient material gain.

Success wasn't just about financial stability. It was about the strength of character, the strength and flexibility to bounce back from adversity, and the capacity to love and nurture even when one's spirit was bruised. It was about being a symbol of hope in the darkest of times, teaching my children that while money and material things might come and go, the true essence of a person lies in their actions, values, and the love they share.

We began celebrating different kinds of successes. A day when we all sat together, sharing stories and laughter, was successful. A moment when one of my children showcased kindness, empathy, or sheer determination was a triumph. In this new world, success was about growth, love, understanding, and the strength of our bond.

This reinvention wasn't just for my children. It was a salve for my own soul, a reminder that my worth wasn't tied to worldly possessions or societal benchmarks but to the love I gave, the lessons I imparted, and the strength I showcased.

Building Resilience for Two

Single motherhood is like walking a tightrope. On one side is the personal journey of healing and rebuilding, and on the other is the responsibility of nurturing and guiding young souls. Every step taken isn't just for oneself but for the young lives that closely follow behind.

In the aftermath of the ordeal, resilience became my most cherished ally. But it wasn't just about my resilience; it was about instilling the same mettle in my children, preparing them for the world, not by shielding them from challenges but by equipping them to face them.

Every conversation we had, every story I shared about my day or my feelings, became an opportunity to teach. Not with preachy lessons but with real-life examples. When I spoke of my struggles, I ensured they also heard about the tiny victories. When I shared tales of despair, they also learned about hope and the relentless spirit of perseverance.

But building resilience isn't just about tales of overcoming challenges. It's also about fostering a safe environment where emotions are acknowledged and validated. An environment where my children felt comfortable sharing their fears, dreams, failures, and triumphs, knowing they would be met with understanding and guidance.

As days turned into weeks and weeks into months, I saw the fruits of this resilience-building. My children, while empathetic to our situation, showcased a strength and maturity beyond their years. They took life's ups and downs in stride, demonstrating an understanding that adversity is but a phase, and with the right attitude, one can emerge stronger.

In our shared journey, resilience wasn't just a trait; it became a way of life. It was in the quiet determination with which we approached each day, the hope that twinkled in our eyes, and the unspoken promise that no matter how tough the climb, we would face it together, drawing strength from each other.

CHAPTER 7

FINANCIAL REBUILDING

*"Do not be embarrassed by your failures,
learn from them and start again."*

— Richard Branson

The Spiritual Side of Money

In our progress towards financial rebuilding, it's crucial to address a vital aspect often overlooked: the spiritual side of money and the concept of abundance. My path to financial recovery was not just about balancing sheets or accumulating assets; it was a deep dive into understanding the energy of money and shifting from a scarcity mindset to one of abundance.

Growing up, my relationship with money was underscored by limitations. The beliefs that resources were scarce, that money was hard to come by, and that saving every penny was the only way to financial security were deeply ingrained in me. However, this journey of financial rebuilding opened my eyes to a transformative truth—money isn't just a currency; it's an energy, and our mindset towards it can significantly influence how it flows into our lives.

The concept of a wealth mindset was a revelation to me. It meant looking at money not as a scarce resource but as an abundant, flowing energy that can be attracted and multiplied. This mindset shift was about believing that there is more than enough for everyone and that prosperity is not just about accumulation but also about contribution and circulation.

I learned that my financial struggles were partially rooted in my own limiting beliefs about money. I had to unlearn the scarcity mindset that was passed down through generations and instead embrace the idea that abundance is a state of being. It was about understanding that wealth isn't defined by the numbers in a bank account but by a sense of sufficiency and the ability to live a fulfilling life.

My journey also led me to explore the Law of Attraction in relation to wealth. I discovered that our thoughts, emotions, and beliefs about money can attract similar experiences. If we focus on lack, we attract scarcity. Conversely, focusing on abundance and gratitude invites more prosperity into our lives. I began practicing gratitude for every financial blessing, no matter how small, and visualized a life of abundance. This wasn't wishful thinking, but a deliberate act of aligning my mindset with the flow of wealth.

Practical Steps to Cultivate a Wealth Mindset

1. **Gratitude and Affirmations**: I started each day by expressing gratitude to God or a Higher Power for what I had, affirming that I was in the flow of abundance. Phrases like "I am open to financial abundance" or "Money flows to me easily and effortlessly" became part of my daily routine.

2. **Education and Understanding**: Learning about financial management, investments, and ways to create passive income was crucial. Understanding money demystified it and made it less daunting.
3. **Generosity and Circulation**: I learned the importance of circulating money. Generosity in spending and giving within my means reinforced my belief in the abundance of the Universe.
4. **Mindful Spending**: Being mindful of my spending habits, focusing on value rather than just cost, and understanding the difference between wants and needs reshaped my financial practices.
5. **Networking with Like-Minded People**: Surrounding myself with people who had a positive outlook on wealth and abundance further reinforced my new mindset.

In essence, rebuilding my financial life was as much about dollars and cents as it was about reshaping my inner beliefs and attitudes towards money. Money is a tool for empowerment, a medium to achieve dreams, and an energy that reflects our internal state. Embracing a wealth mindset transformed not just my bank balance but my entire approach to life. It's a testament that when we change our thoughts about money, we invite the abundance that is waiting to flow into our lives.

Recognizing Money Mindset Blocks

The treacherous path of the scam didn't merely rob me of my savings; it threatened to imprison me in a cage of insecurity and self-doubt. That cage, however, wasn't constructed overnight.

Looking back, I could see its foundation was laid much earlier, influenced by my complicated relationship with money.

Money is more than just a transactional tool. It's a mirror reflecting our innermost beliefs, fears, and values. My discomfort with money was palpable, casting shadows over every financial decision I made. When my coffers were full, a nagging fear whispered, reminding me of the impermanence of this abundance. And when they were empty, the familiar pangs of worry echoed louder, mocking my inability to preserve and grow.

This mindset—the constant fear of loss even when abundant and the relentless worry in scarcity—revealed a deep-seated lack mentality. A mindset where money was perceived more as a fleeting guest rather than a trusted ally. My habitual generosity further complicated this relationship. While giving is virtuous, the extreme selflessness where one's own needs are consistently overlooked hinted at an underlying belief: perhaps I felt I wasn't deserving of wealth or prosperity.

Recognizing these blocks was a revelation. It wasn't merely about being cheated out of money; it was about confronting years of accumulated beliefs that perhaps made me vulnerable in the first place. The realization was clear; to rebuild financially, I first had to dismantle these limiting beliefs brick by brick.

Strategies for Financial Recovery

Embarking on the path of financial recovery, I realized that resilience and diligence were crucial, but they needed to be anchored in a sound strategy. My encounter with a significant debt of more than $190,000 was daunting, yet it presented an opportunity to transform my relationship with money and embrace a future grounded in security and abundance.

It wasn't about merely recouping losses; it was about embracing a new philosophy regarding wealth. Informed by experts like Dave Ramsey and the Barefoot Investor, I gained valuable insights. But rather than solely focusing on their methods, I tailored a strategy that resonated with my newfound understanding of money as an energetic and abundant resource.

Budgeting became an essential tool in my arsenal. It was more than tracking expenses; it was about consciously and deliberately directing energy (money) towards my goals and needs, ensuring a balance between debt repayment and the well-being of my family. Even as I meticulously budgeted, I was mindful to infuse this process with gratitude and respect for money's role in our lives.

Building an emergency fund was another critical step. This fund was not just a financial buffer but a symbol of stability and preparedness, integral to fostering a sense of security and peace of mind.

The commitment to work multiple jobs was underpinned by a clear purpose. Each extra hour of work, each moment of sacrifice, was not just about earning more but about manifesting my commitment to financial freedom and abundance. This period taught me invaluable lessons in discipline, the beauty of delayed gratification, and the joy of achieving hard-earned goals.

Yet, the most profound shift occurred when I explored the spiritual dimension of money. I began to perceive money as a form of energy that responds to respect, value, and gratitude. This perspective shifted my approach from merely accumulating wealth to understanding and harnessing its true potential. I learned to approach money not with a mindset of scarcity but with one of abundance, where respect for money meant engaging with it in a mindful, purposeful manner.

As I navigated this journey, each debt cleared was not just a financial milestone but a step towards reestablishing my self-worth and confidence. It was a testament to my belief in life's abundance and a reaffirmation of my trust in the Universe. This journey was more than financial recovery; it was an awakening to a life where wealth is not just about the balance in your bank account but the richness of your relationship with money and the abundance it brings.

Navigating the aftermath of the scam, I found myself in a situation where financial resources were limited. However, this period of financial constraint became a gateway to a pivotal revelation: living with mindful spending wasn't about scarcity but about intelligent prioritization and innovative resourcefulness.

With the looming challenge of debt, my relationship with money took a significant turn. Each dollar I spent became an integral part of my journey towards financial stability. This shifted my perspective from viewing my budget as a limitation to seeing it as an opportunity for creativity and resource maximization.

The journey began with distinguishing essential needs from desirable wants. While it was challenging to let go of certain luxuries and comforts, the focus shifted to essentials: securing our home, providing nutritious meals, and maintaining a nurturing environment for my children. This phase highlighted the essence of living a fulfilling life, not just existing. We were not merely getting by; we were mastering the art of flourishing within our means.

Resourcefulness became a key theme in our daily lives. From finding new purposes for old items to DIY solutions and exploring cost-effective alternatives, our goal was clear—derive the maximum value from every dollar spent. Meals were transformed into home-cooked, wholesome experiences that also fostered quality family time. Entertainment shifted from costly activities to appreciating life's simpler pleasures—enjoying a board game at home, exploring the beauty of nature, or a cozy movie night with homemade snacks.

This phase of mindful spending also imparted essential life lessons to my children about the true value of money. They learned that genuine contentment and happiness are not solely dependent on lavish expenditures but can be discovered in modest settings when love and appreciation for what we have are at the forefront.

In essence, this chapter of our lives was not about navigating a path of scarcity but about embracing a mindset of abundance, where joy, love, and satisfaction were found in the mindful and purposeful use of our resources. It was a testament to the fact that abundance isn't just about the wealth we accumulate but about the richness of our experiences and the gratitude with which we embrace life's journey.

Building a Sustainable and Empowered Financial Future

Emerging from a financial crisis, especially one as crippling as the scam that derailed my life, meant more than just repaying debts. It was about crafting a future where financial stability wasn't just a distant dream but a tangible, achievable reality.

This journey of empowerment began with education. While I had previously been hesitant and insecure about money, I now consumed knowledge voraciously. Books, seminars, online courses—any source that could offer insights into financial wisdom became a resource. It wasn't just about making money but about understanding it, respecting it, and mastering its dynamics.

Investing became the next frontier. With the debts cleared, the money saved wasn't just stashed away but was put to work. Through calculated risks and informed decisions, I delved into investments that promised growth, not just immediate returns. This shift from a short-term survival mindset to a long-term growth perspective was pivotal.

Simultaneously, there was an emphasis on building multiple streams of income. No longer was I willing to place all my eggs in one basket. By diversifying income sources, I aimed to create a safety net, ensuring that if one source faltered, others could provide the necessary support.

Yet, building a sustainable financial future wasn't just a solitary endeavor. Ensuring my children were equipped with financial literacy became paramount. They were taught the value of savings, the importance of smart spending, and the potential of investments. By imparting this knowledge, I was ensuring that they would be better prepared to face the financial challenges and opportunities of their future.

The journey from financial ruin to empowerment was both challenging and enlightening. With each hurdle crossed and each goal achieved, I was not only building a secure financial future but was also crafting a legacy—a legacy of resilience, wisdom, and empowered financial independence for generations to come.

CHAPTER 8

DELIBERATE ACTION AND TRANSFORMATION

"The journey of a thousand miles begins with one step."

— Lao Tzu

Harnessing the Power of Intention

Every journey of transformation begins with a single, powerful catalyst—intention. Unlike fleeting desires or short-lived resolutions, intention runs deeper. It is a deliberate commitment we make to ourselves, a force that propels us toward genuine change.

During the lowest moments of my life, amidst the financial chaos and emotional turmoil, there was a quiet voice within that refused to be silenced. It whispered of hope and resilience. It wasn't just about wanting to change or hoping for a better day; it was about setting a conscious intention to rebuild, no matter the odds. This intention wasn't born out of desperation but from a place of empowered choice.

Intention, however, is more than mere thought. It is the heart's deepest wish combined with the mind's clarity. It's the alignment of our internal compass towards our true north. By harnessing its power, we can manifest our goals and dreams into reality.

One might ask, how does one harness the power of intention? First, it's about clarity. You need to be precise about what you want. In my case, the goal was to bounce back, to repay every debt, to rebuild my life, and to ensure my children's future was secure. These weren't vague aspirations; they were specific targets.

Next, intention requires emotion. It's the passion, the heart's fire, that transforms a mere thought into an unwavering intention. The emotional intensity I felt was raw—a blend of pain from the past and hope for the future. This emotion was the fuel that kept the flame of intention burning bright.

Finally, intention thrives on action. Without deliberate steps towards realization, even the most robust intention remains a dormant seed. I not only set intentions but also charted out clear steps to achieve them—be it financial planning, self-education, or emotional healing.

In the grand narrative of life, intention is the thread that weaves our dreams into reality. By harnessing its power, we can initiate the most profound transformations, turning adversities into stepping stones and setbacks into comebacks.

With a strong intention as the foundation, the next pivotal phase in transformation is action. Yet not just any action—it's about deliberate, focused, and strategic steps that align with the end goal. It's about charting a new path forward.

As I looked at the rubble of my past, it was evident that retracing old steps wouldn't suffice. A new blueprint was needed—one that was built on lessons learned, new insights, and a vision of a better future. This wasn't just about rectifying past mistakes but about pioneering a new trajectory.

The initial stages of this process were introspective. I pondered the choices that led me to the past crisis. While it was tempting to linger in regret, the objective was clear—to glean wisdom from past experiences. Each misstep was dissected, not for self-reproach but for enlightenment. Understanding the 'whys' of the past paved the way for the 'hows' of the future.

Having garnered these insights, the next step was setting milestones. While the ultimate goal might be monumental, breaking it down into smaller, achievable tasks made it less daunting. Each milestone, when achieved, not only brought me closer to my goal but also bolstered confidence and reignited hope.

But charting a new path isn't a solitary endeavor. Along the way, I sought mentors, joined communities, and collaborated with like-minded souls. This created a support system, a collective energy that propelled me forward. Sharing stories, learning from others' journeys, and basking in mutual encouragement enriched my path with varied perspectives and invaluable wisdom.

Equally vital in this journey was adaptability. While the blueprint served as a guide, I was attuned to life's unpredictable nature. When faced with unexpected obstacles or new opportunities, the ability to adapt, recalibrate, and pivot was paramount. This flexibility ensured that I remained on course, even when the winds of change tried to sway me.

In essence, charting a new path forward is a dynamic dance between planning and adaptability, between individual effort and collective support, and between learning from the past and innovating for the future. By embarking on this journey with a blend of determination and openness, transformation becomes not just a possibility but an inevitable reality.

The Power of Perspective

The Half-Full Glass: Embracing Optimism

Life's like a tall glass of water. You've probably heard the age-old question: is the glass half empty or half full? It's a simple way to determine one's perspective on life. While the amount of water remains constant, it's how we choose to view it that makes all the difference.

Remember when I took on the mammoth challenge of climbing the Q1 Tower? The climb was both literal and metaphorical. I could've focused on the sweat, the heart pounding out of my chest, or the heights that induced fear. Instead, I chose to view each deliberate step as one step closer to the top. That's the half-full glass in action.

Optimism, or seeing the glass as half full, is a way to acknowledge the positive amidst the negative, even when life's challenges seem insurmountable. It's a transformative power that enables us to face adversity head-on, knowing that the situation can and will improve. By focusing on the potential, the positive, and the possibilities, we open doors to solutions, creativity, and growth.

We've been taught that failure is bad, a mark of inadequacy. But what if we've been looking at it all wrong? What if failure wasn't a dead end but a detour sign leading us to a better route?

My experiences, especially the scam ordeal, serve as a powerful illustration of this philosophy. In the face of deceit and betrayal, I could've viewed myself as a victim, bogged down by the weight of despair. Instead, I saw it as an awakening, a life lesson handed to me in a rather rough package. I chose to rise from it stronger, wiser, and more tenacious than ever.

By redefining failure, we shift our focus from the setback itself to the lessons it offers. We begin to see every misstep as an opportunity for growth, every defeat as a bridge to success, and every heartbreak as a chance to rebuild, stronger and better.

Sometimes, the biggest change comes not from altering our circumstances but from altering our vantage point. Life will always be riddled with challenges, but by shifting our viewpoint, we can transform obstacles into opportunities.

Consider the story of my participation in the community project with my friends Mark and Michelle. It was an experience that pushed me out of my comfort zone, allowing me to face and conquer my fears. It wasn't just about giving back; it was about personal growth, connection, and breaking barriers. I could have seen it as a simple charitable endeavor, but I chose to see it as an enriching journey of self-discovery.

Shifting our viewpoint is like adjusting the focus on a camera. What was once blurry becomes clear. We start to notice the silver linings, the unexpected joys, and the hidden opportunities in every challenge. It's a reminder that, often, the most profound changes arise not from altering the scene before us but from viewing it through a different lens.

In conclusion, perspective is an immensely powerful tool. It shapes our reality, influences our reactions, and determines our outcomes. From the optimism of a half-full glass to the transformative lessons hidden in failures to the enlightening revelations from a shifted viewpoint, it's evident that how we choose to see things can make all the difference. The stories of climbing towers, overcoming scams, and community involvement are not just tales of events but narratives of perspective. Embrace the power of perspective, and I embrace the power to change my world.

Small Actions, Monumental Changes

The transformative journey isn't always characterized by grand gestures or sweeping changes. Often, it's the minute, everyday decisions and actions that culminate in the most profound shifts in our lives. Each small step, taken with determination and intention, compounds over time, leading to monumental changes.

Reflecting on my journey, I wasn't catapulted to the zenith of recovery overnight. It wasn't one sweeping move that eradicated the pains and scars of the scam ordeal. Instead, it was a plethora of tiny, consistent efforts that shaped my comeback story. Just as a mosaic masterpiece is composed of innumerable individual tiles, my renewed life was crafted through countless minor yet significant actions.

Consider the power of discipline. Waking up an hour earlier every day might seem trivial in isolation. But when you persist over a year, it results in 365 additional hours—equivalent to fifteen full days. I utilized such extra hours for self-education, meditation, and planning. The knowledge gained, peace attained, and strategies devised during these hours were instrumental in my financial and emotional recovery.

Then there's the strength of habit. Adopting a simple habit, like daily journaling or setting aside a small portion of income for savings and investing, can have transformative outcomes. Over months and years, journal entries morph into a treasure trove of insights, and modest savings burgeon into a significant safety net.

Moreover, these small actions serve another critical purpose—they foster a mindset of empowerment. Every time you choose to act, even in the tiniest capacity, you are reaffirming your agency over circumstances. You're sending a message to yourself: "I am in control. I can influence outcomes." This nurtures self-belief, which in turn propels you to undertake more significant actions.

In essence, while the allure of massive, immediate change is tempting, it's the dedication to small, consistent actions that crafts a resilient and enduring transformation. They serve as constant reminders that every effort, no matter how minuscule, is a brick in the edifice of our success story.

The Art of Proactive Living

Waiting for circumstances to change or for fate to smile is a passive existence. True transformation demands an active, proactive stance, where you don't merely react to life's events but shape them.

Being proactive means seizing the reins of your destiny. It's about anticipating challenges, planning, and acting in the present to manifest desired outcomes. It's a shift from a mindset of "Why is this happening to me?" to "How can I make this work for me?"

During the tumultuous phase post-scam, I could have succumbed to desolation, allowing events to dictate my emotional and financial state. But a proactive approach, rooted in my mother's wisdom and my intrinsic fortitude, altered the trajectory. Instead of waiting for a miracle, I became the architect of my recovery.

A proactive stance involves cultivating foresight. By continually educating oneself, seeking mentorship, and staying updated, one can predict potential pitfalls and opportunities. This foresight enabled me to devise strategies not just for immediate recovery but also for long-term growth.

Being proactive also entails establishing boundaries and setting priorities. After the ordeal, my priorities were crystal clear: emotional healing, financial recovery, and ensuring my children's well-being. With these priorities as my compass, I could make informed choices, even when inundated with multiple demands.

Lastly, proactivity is about ownership. It's about owning your decisions, mistakes, successes, and lessons. By embracing this sense of responsibility, you are empowered to drive change rather than being at its mercy.

In a world that's in perpetual flux, a proactive approach is the anchor that ensures you remain the captain of your ship, navigating through storms and sunshine alike towards the horizon of your aspirations.

CHAPTER 9

LIFE'S TRUE WEALTH

"The real measure of our wealth is how much we'd be worth if we lost all our money."

— J.H. Jowett

Valuing Non-Material Blessings

In a world dominated by materialistic pursuits, there exists an undercurrent of life's true treasures that don't come with price tags. These are the blessings of life that can't be quantified in monetary terms yet hold immeasurable value in the context of a meaningful life. The simple joy of a child's laughter, the solace in a loved one's embrace, or the sheer wonder of a sunset can be profound reminders of the richness life offers beyond material possessions.

In moments of hardship, like the one I faced, there is often an unspoken gift—a realization of what truly matters. It's not uncommon for people to equate success and contentment with wealth and possessions. But when these are stripped away, as they were in my case, a more profound truth emerges. As I journeyed through adversity, the intangible blessings—love, support, faith, and inner strength—became the pillars on which I rebuilt my life.

Single moments carry with them the weight of timeless memories. Think of the days when, despite the weight of the world on my shoulders, I still managed to make my children laugh, or when I felt the warmth of my community rallying behind me. These moments might not have monetary value, but they're priceless in the treasure chest of memories.

Embracing non-material blessings involves a shift in perspective. It requires recognizing the value of experiences over possessions, relationships over riches, and moments over materials. When I start to see wealth as a combination of the love I give and receive, the memories I create, and the lives I touch, the entire definition of prosperity undergoes a profound transformation.

The Transformative Power of Gratitude

Gratitude, often understated, is a potent tool for transformation. It's the gentle whisper that reminds us of the good, even when shadows loom large. In my journey, gratitude wasn't just a coping mechanism; it was a catalyst for transformation.

Studies have consistently shown the positive impact of gratitude on mental well-being. Those who regularly practice gratitude by taking time to notice and reflect upon the things they're thankful for experience more positive emotions, feel more alive, sleep better, and even have stronger immune systems. But beyond these benefits, gratitude provides a perspective shift—from what's lacking to what's abundant in our lives.

My story reflects this shift profoundly. While facing financial setbacks, I still found reasons to be grateful—the strength I discovered in myself, the unwavering support of my mother, the love and resilience of my children, and the lessons I learned along the way. Each of these factors, acknowledged through a lens of gratitude, provided a counterbalance to the challenges I faced.

Gratitude doesn't deny the hardships or the pain. Instead, it offers a broader view of life, acknowledging the bad while also spotlighting the good. It's akin to looking at a tapestry—while there might be dark threads, they are woven in with vibrant colors, together creating a beautiful picture.

In my deliberate climb, gratitude was like the checkpoints that provided moments of respite, reflection, and rejuvenation. By focusing on life's blessings, big or small, I not only coped with my adversities but transformed them into catalysts towards a richer, more meaningful life.

To harness the transformative power of gratitude, one doesn't need grand gestures. Simple practices such as maintaining a gratitude journal, expressing thanks to loved ones, or even taking a moment each day to reflect on one's blessings can create ripples of positive change. As you've discovered, when faced with storms, gratitude is the compass that points towards hope, resilience, and a wealth that transcends material confines.

Nurturing Deep Connections

In the ebb and flow of life, amidst the chase for material accomplishments, there's a fundamental truth that often remains obscured: the core of human existence is about connections. It's the bonds we form, the relationships we cherish, and the depth of our interactions that truly define the richness of our lives.

My journey, with its peaks and troughs, taught me the significance of nurturing these connections. When the world seemed to crumble around me, it was the unwavering support of my mother, the innocence and trust of my children, and the backing of supportive friends and a community that held me steady. These relationships didn't just offer solace; they formed the bedrock of my resilience and eventual triumph.

But why are these deep connections so essential? They act as mirrors, reflecting our strengths when we're blinded by our vulnerabilities. They provide a safety net, ensuring we never truly hit rock bottom. They celebrate our successes, amplify our joys, and divide our sorrows. They are life's true anchors, providing stability amidst chaos.

To nurture these connections requires conscious effort. It means prioritizing relationships over routines, making time for heart-to-heart conversations, and being there in moments of need and moments of joy. It means being vulnerable, opening up about your fears and hopes, and allowing others to do the same. It's about creating a space of trust, empathy, and unconditional love.

My story is a tribute to the power of these deep connections. When faced with adversity, I wasn't alone; I was surrounded by a circle of love and trust, which gave me the strength to rise. And as I moved forward, these connections deepened, for adversity has a way of crystallizing what truly matters. By nurturing these bonds, I didn't just recover; I flourished, drawing strength from these profound relationships.

The Abundance in Everyday Moments

Often, in the pursuit of grand milestones and life-altering experiences, we overlook the magic tucked away in everyday moments. Yet, it's in these seemingly mundane instances that the essence of life often reveals itself. A smile shared, an unexpected word of encouragement, the simple joy of a home-cooked meal, or even the tranquility of a quiet evening spent with loved ones—these moments, though fleeting, carry with them an abundance that's both profound and transformative.

This path has taught me to recognize and cherish this abundance. When faced with the scam ordeal, every day brought its set of challenges. Yet, it was the daily acts of love, kindness, and perseverance that pieced together my path to recovery. The morning routines with the children, the conversations with my mother, the moments of reflection and prayer, and the daily grind to rebuild my life—each of these seemingly ordinary moments held within them seeds of extraordinary resilience and hope.

Life's true wealth isn't always about the landmark events; it's often found in the intervals in between. It's in the laughter shared over a simple joke, the warmth of a hug after a tiring day, the satisfaction of a job well done, or the comfort of familiar routines. It's in recognizing the beauty of the present, understanding that every moment holds within it the potential for joy, love, and abundance.

The beauty of everyday moments is that they're accessible to all. They don't demand grand gestures or monumental efforts. All they require is awareness—a conscious decision to be present, to engage fully with the moment and to recognize the abundance it offers. By doing so, you transform the ordinary into the extraordinary, turning everyday moments into treasures of joy, gratitude, and profound meaning.

In my story, this abundance in everyday moments was a beacon of light, guiding me through the darkest times. It taught me that even when faced with overwhelming challenges, there's always a reservoir of hope, love, and abundance available—if only we pause, recognize, and cherish it.

Kindness & Empathy

Life can sometimes throw us curveballs, catching us off guard. In those moments, simple acts of kindness and understanding can serve as a guiding light. When I was tangled up in the scam, what I was really seeking was a real connection, a genuine heart-to-heart. Isn't it something we all crave deep down? A feeling that someone, somewhere, truly cares about us.

But here's where it gets interesting. After the storm of the scam passed, kindness and empathy shined even brighter. It's tough to get back up when you've been knocked down hard. That's when you need to show yourself some kindness. It's essential to remember that it wasn't my fault. Everyone can make mistakes when they're chasing genuine human connection.

And it's not just about the kindness I show to myself but also the kindness others show me. A simple "I'm here for you" or "I understand what you're going through" can mean the world. This shows that you're not alone in this big world. There's always someone willing to lend a shoulder or offer a comforting word.

My journey, with its ups and downs, teaches us a big lesson. Even when faced with betrayal, we can choose love over hate, understanding over blame. This choice, though it might seem small, can work wonders. It can turn a painful memory into a stepping stone towards a better future.

To wrap it up, while money and fancy things might be lost, the treasure of kindness and understanding is ours forever. They are the real gems in life. When everything else is uncertain, these two virtues guide us, help us heal, and remind us of who we truly are. My story inspires all of us to cherish and spread these gems, lighting up not just our path but also the paths of those around us.

CHAPTER 10

EMBRACING ORDER IN LIFE

"In all chaos, there is a cosmos, in all disorder a secret order."

— Carl Jung

Find Order in Chaos

Life is like a song. Even when it gets confusing or tough, there's a beat to it. Nature shows us this every day. When the sun rises and sets, or the waves come and go, or even when butterflies fly from place to place, they all tell us one thing: there's a plan, even when stuff seems crazy.

In the wake of a scam that turned my world upside down, I encountered another daunting challenge: a car accident that shattered the illusion of control we often feel we possess. In that scary moment, when both cars crashed with loud noises and broken pieces, everything felt so slow, like the time it takes for day to turn into night.

After the chaos, the aftermath of the accident painted a scene of utter devastation, similar to flowers that bloom and then quickly fade away. Here today, gone tomorrow. But, in the middle of all this mess, I met someone special—a nun who looked peaceful even when everything around was going wrong.

The scene was eerily quiet following the loudness of the crash. Amidst the silent alarm of onlookers, the nun stepped out from the other car, her face calm, eyes filled with a deep understanding, and lips murmuring a silent prayer. With her habit flowing gracefully around her, she appeared as a timeless emblem amidst modern chaos.

She approached me, her steps measured and steady. "Are you okay?" she asked. Her voice was soft and soothing, akin to the sound of leaves in the wind.

I nodded, still in shock. "I'm so sorry," I began, but she raised a hand to stop me.

"This is just a tiny part of life's big picture," she said. "You see," she continued, gesturing around, "nature has its storms, its wildfires, its disruptions. Yet, the sun still rises, and life finds its way. The rhythm of nature isn't in its perfection but its resilience." Life's song isn't about always being perfect but about bouncing back.

Her words resonated deeply. It wasn't just about the accident anymore but about every challenge, every disruption I had faced or would face in life. The scam, the setbacks, the hurdles were but notes in the grand composition of my life, essential for the crescendo that awaited.

The nun's perspective was a revelation. She was the embodiment of understanding this rhythm of life. Despite the fresh trauma, she remained grounded, anchored in her faith, and understanding of life's larger rhythm, akin to a mighty oak standing tall amidst a storm.

With our paths crossing briefly, she left an indelible mark on my journey. The rhythm of nature she spoke of became a guiding principle. It reminded me that adversities are but seasons of life, and just as winter makes way for spring, challenges pave the path for growth and rejuvenation.

In our lives, we often seek control, but nature teaches us the beauty of surrender and resilience. The key isn't to resist or control every change but to find our rhythm within it, to dance to the tune of life, and to understand that there's a melody, a purpose, even in the most discordant notes.

As I moved forward, I began to see not just the challenges but the spaces between them, the rhythm that guides us back to our path, the symphony that plays through our highs and lows. Life, I realized, isn't about avoiding the storms but learning to find our rhythm through them.

In the dizzying aftermath of the accident, a singular thought played on repeat in my mind: "The first law of heaven is order." While the scam had left my mind muddled and distracted, the accident spotlighted the consequences of such disarray. Thoughts influence actions, and when one's mind is in disarray, it often leads to unanticipated and regrettable outcomes.

Reflecting on this, I considered how our thoughts, when organized and clear, can amplify our actions. Just as a musician must know the notes and their sequence to create a symphony, so too must we structure our thoughts to manifest our desired outcomes in life.

In the wake of the accident, I was a living testament to the power of structured thinking. Though traumatized, I recognized the need to process the event methodically. I acknowledged the emotional weight of both the scam and the accident and sought professional and spiritual help to navigate these turbulent waters. Taking time out, seeking help from within, and attending therapy provided a structure, a framework within with which I could organize my thoughts, understand my emotions, and chart a course forward.

I also found clarity in the wisdom of the nun. Her calm amidst the storm was a result of structured thought processes developed over years of discipline and faith. This realization served as a guidepost, guiding me toward a mindset where organized thought could lead to amplified, purposeful action. It became evident that embracing order in one's mind could transform chaos into clarity and trauma into lessons of strength and resilience.

Mindfulness & Meditation

In the harmony of life, it is all too easy to get lost in the hustle and bustle of every day. With my life experiences echoing in the background, I've come to realize that amidst the chaos, finding moments of stillness is essential. Much like pausing to inhale a fresh breath of air after a long underwater dive, mindfulness and meditation act as lifesavers in the sea of life's challenges.

Mindfulness: It's more than just a buzzword. It's the practice of being fully present and engaged in the current moment without judgment. It's about grounding oneself in the here and now. Research, including a significant study from Harvard University, has shown that mindfulness practices can literally rewire our brains, leading to improved focus, reduced symptoms of anxiety and depression, and better overall well-being.

Connecting this to my journey, I think back to the days in Samoa when challenges were as frequent as the waves hitting the shores. It would have been so easy to be swept away, to drown in the challenges. But practicing mindfulness, even unconsciously, was akin to anchoring myself to the sturdy trunk of a palm tree amidst a storm. It provided the strength and clarity to see things as they were, not worse than they were.

Meditation, on the other hand, serves as a deeper dive into the mind. Think of it as an intimate date with oneself, a chance to listen to the innermost thoughts and feelings. A study published in the journal *Psychological Science* found that meditation enhances one's ability to regulate emotions and even improves memory and cognitive functions.

While the benefits sound appealing, how did it apply in the context of my life? Each traumatic event, every moment of pain, could have left indelible scars. Yet, it was through meditation that I learned the art of healing. Meditative practices helped unpack the baggage of the past gently, one memory at a time. It wasn't about forgetting but about understanding, accepting, and eventually finding peace.

Interestingly, the power of mindfulness and meditation is amplified when combined. A study from the *Journal of Cognitive Enhancement* suggests that combining these two practices can lead to improved attention and overall well-being, and the effects can be long-lasting.

So, how can one embark on this transformative journey?

1. Start Simple: As with any new endeavor, it's essential to start small. Begin with a five-minute meditation session daily. As time progresses and comfort grows, gradually increase the duration.
2. Embrace the Present: When practicing mindfulness, engage all the senses. For instance, if you're sipping a cup of tea, relish its warmth, inhale its aroma, taste its flavor. Be wholly present in that act.
3. Guided Meditations: For beginners, guided meditations—available abundantly online—can be a great starting point. They provide direction and can make the process less daunting.
4. Consistency Is Key: Just as watering a plant daily helps it grow, consistent practice will cultivate a resilient mind.
5. Reflect on Personal Experiences: Relate the calm and clarity from the practices to challenging life situations. Over time, this will cultivate an intrinsic motivation to continue.

My voyage, intertwined with life's highs and lows, has been significantly enriched by mindfulness and meditation. These practices are not just coping mechanisms but powerful tools to enhance life's quality, grounding us during storms and elevating our spirits during calm. They act as bridges, helping us traverse from painful memories to a place of healing and understanding. After all, in the grand tapestry of life, self-care isn't a luxury; it's a necessity. Embrace it, celebrate it, and let the mind find its serene oasis.

Foundations of Strength

Life's odyssey is a rich collage of experiences intertwined with strands of emotions, challenges, and triumphs. Among these threads, our physical well-being stands out as one of the most vital. The strength of our body often directly impacts the toughness of our mind, becoming the foundation upon which our mental fortitude is built.

My sail, too, like many others, was punctuated by moments of intense fear and anxiety. There came a time when I discovered a lump in my breast. The mere thought of it being malignant was paralyzing. I felt the walls closing in, and an abyss of fear threatened to consume me. The 'what-ifs' loomed large, casting a shadow over every joyous moment. I hesitated to get it tested, afraid of confronting a reality that might shatter my world.

However, as days turned to weeks, the internal turmoil became unbearable. The uncertainty was corrosive, eating away at my peace of mind. Gathering every ounce of courage, I decided to face my fears head-on. I went for the test. Those waiting moments felt like an eternity, but when the results returned negative, a flood of relief washed over me, renewing my zest for life. It was a stark reminder of the fragility and preciousness of life. From that moment, I pledged to prioritize my health, both inside and out, realizing that nurturing our body is paramount to nurturing our spirit.

The link between physical health and mental resilience cannot be understated. When our bodies are fit and healthy, we're better equipped to handle emotional challenges and mental stress. Engaging in regular physical activities, even as simple as walking or stretching, releases endorphins. Often called the 'feel-good' hormones, they act as nature's painkillers, uplifting our mood and combating feelings of depression or anxiety.

Furthermore, maintaining a balanced diet ensures that our body gets essential nutrients, which directly impacts our cognitive functions and emotional well-being. A study from the University of Warwick showed that consuming fruits and vegetables regularly not only enhances our physical health but also our mental well-being, leading to higher life satisfaction.

Fitness routines also inculcate discipline, consistency, and goal setting, traits that bolster mental resilience. Each time we overcome the resistance to skip a workout or choose a nutritious meal over junk food, we're training our minds to face challenges and make beneficial choices.

Wellness goes beyond mere physical fitness. It's an integrated process of conscious choices towards a more holistic and fulfilling life. This encompasses mental, emotional, and even spiritual practices that nourish our inner selves.

Reflecting upon my experience, the emotional turbulence I faced was a result of neglecting the signals my body was sending. The fear and anxiety were not just about the lump; they were an accumulation of not listening to what my body needed. The revelation following that testing was not just about the absence of a disease; it was a profound awakening to the importance of self-care.

In essence, our bodies are the temples that house our spirit. Just as a temple needs upkeep, our bodies require care and attention, too. Physical well-being is not just about looking good; it's about feeling good. When we're at our physical best, we're also mentally sharper, emotionally balanced, and better prepared to face life's adversities.

Listen to your body. It whispers so you don't have to hear it scream. Take that walk, eat that fruit, drink that water, and get that check-up. Your body reflects your journey, your struggles and victories. Honor it, cherish it, and most importantly, take care of it. Your mental endurance depends on it. The road towards a healthier you is progress towards a stronger, more enduring you. Embrace it with open arms, and watch how life transforms in beautiful, unexpected ways.

Relationships and Boundaries

Relationships, mirroring the intricate dance of planets around the sun, thrive in a delicate balance, dictated by invisible boundaries. This cosmic choreography ensures harmony and prevents collisions. Similarly, our interpersonal relationships flourish when we understand and respect boundaries.

The car incident I was involved in with the nun was a stark reminder of what happens when boundaries, both literal and metaphorical, aren't recognized in time. The physical boundaries on the road were transgressed, leading to a collision. But in the aftermath, a different set of boundaries came into play. The nun, with her graceful calm, offered prayers. She could've responded with anger or blame, but she chose compassion, respecting the emotional boundaries that such a traumatic situation necessitates.

It made me introspect on how often we, in our relationships, overstep or don't define boundaries. These boundaries aren't barriers; they're definitions that provide clarity. They help us understand where we end, and another begins. Such clarity is essential, especially when navigating the aftermath of traumas such as the scam I experienced. When boundaries are blurred, it's easy to project our pain onto others or allow them to overstep and deepen our wounds.

By setting and respecting boundaries, we create a safe space for mutual growth and understanding. They enable open communication, ensure mutual respect, and most importantly, they protect the sanctity of individual experiences while fostering collective growth.

Embracing Uncertainty with Structure

Life, by its very nature, is a vast expanse of uncertainties. One moment, you're driving on a clear path, and the next, you're confronting an unforeseen challenge, comparable to a car hurtling towards you. But how we respond to these uncertainties often defines our journey.

The scam left me disoriented, an emotional whirlwind with no semblance of order. This lack of internal structure made the subsequent car accident even more jarring. However, the aftermath of the accident became a classroom for understanding the significance of structure amidst uncertainty.

It wasn't about the accident itself but the coping mechanisms and the support structures that followed. The nun, with her age-old wisdom, offered prayers—a structure that many lean on in times of distress. Her faith was a structured approach to understanding and accepting life's uncertainties. It was a poignant reminder that while we cannot always control external events, we can control our responses to them.

Taking a leaf from that experience, I began to see the power of structured responses. Whether it was seeking therapy after the scam or reaching out to support groups after the accident, these were structured ways to navigate chaos. It's akin to building a shelter during a storm. The storm might rage on, but the structure provides safety.

Moreover, structure isn't always about rigidity. It's about having a framework flexible enough to adapt but robust enough to provide guidance. For instance, having a daily routine can ground us, even when the world around us seems chaotic. Simple acts such as journaling, meditation, or even regular walks can create a semblance of order in an otherwise unpredictable day.

Life will always throw curveballs. But with a structured approach, we can not only catch them, but sometimes even hit them out of the park. Embracing uncertainty with structure allows us to find order in chaos, to find meaning in randomness, and to navigate life's tumultuous seas with a compass of our making.

I hope my personal story serves as a poignant backdrop to explore the deeper nuances of relationships, boundaries, and how a structured approach can be our ally in embracing life's uncertainties. Through this narrative, we can understand that while life's events might be unpredictable, our responses can be crafted with thoughtful intention, ensuring we emerge stronger from every challenge.

CHAPTER 11

EMOTIONAL RESILIENCE

*"Life doesn't get easier or more forgiving;
we get stronger and more resilient."*

— Steve Maraboli

Coping Mechanisms for Turbulent Times

Life is as unpredictable as the ocean's tides. Sometimes, it's calm, peaceful, and beautifully still, and at other times, it's wild, restless, and stormy. Just as sailors equip their ships to weather the fiercest storms, so too must we fortify our emotional resilience to navigate the turbulence of life. This fortification doesn't mean suppressing emotions but rather equipping ourselves with the tools to understand, process, and grow from them.

The aftermath of the scam was an emotional tempest for me. A whirlwind of betrayal, self-doubt, guilt, and a multitude of other emotions threatened to drown my spirit. Yet, it was the deliberate use of specific coping mechanisms that became my life buoy.

Journaling was one such mechanism. Pouring my thoughts and feelings out to God or onto paper provided clarity and catharsis. This practice allowed me to externalize my emotions, giving me a clearer perspective and helping me identify patterns, triggers, and solutions.

Mindfulness and meditation were other invaluable tools. Taking time each day to sit in stillness, focusing on my breath, helped ground me. It created a sanctuary of peace amid the chaos, enabling me to face my emotions head-on and, in the process, gain a deeper understanding of them.

Another key coping strategy was seeking support. Engaging in open conversations with close friends, family, or even professionals offered different perspectives and invaluable advice. Remember, seeking assistance isn't a sign of weakness; it's a sign of strength and self-awareness.

Lastly, setting boundaries was crucial. Recognizing the need for emotional and mental space, especially during trying times, can be incredibly empowering. Be it distancing oneself from negative influences or taking a digital detox, ensuring mental well-being becomes paramount.

It's essential to remember that while these mechanisms provide relief and understanding, it's the cumulative effort of consistently employing them that fortifies emotional resilience over time.

Reframing Negative Narratives

Our reality is shaped not just by events but by the narratives we weave around them. The stories we tell ourselves hold immense power; they can either imprison us in cycles of negativity or propel us towards growth and transformation.

Following the financial devastation, it would have been easy for me to weave a narrative of victimhood. However, such a story would have paralyzed me, preventing any forward movement. Instead, by consciously choosing to reframe the narrative, I found empowerment and a pathway to recovery.

Reframing involves challenging and questioning the validity of our initial reactions. For instance, instead of thinking, "I am a failure because I fell for the scam," I prompted myself to ask, "What lessons can I glean from this experience?" This shift in perspective transforms a negative event into an opportunity for growth.

Another powerful reframing tool is gratitude. Even in the direst situations, there are always elements to be thankful for. In my case, even though I lost money, I still had my health, my children, my skills, and my determination. By focusing on these blessings, the weight of the negative narrative began to lift, making room for expectancy and positivity.

Visualization is also a potent method. Instead of getting mired in the present pain, I visualized a future where I had not only recovered but thrived. This forward-looking approach motivated me, providing a clear goal to strive towards.

Lastly, it's essential to surround oneself with positive influences. Books, uplifting music, motivational speakers, or even positive individuals can help reinforce a constructive narrative. Their stories and messages serve as reminders that setbacks can be springboards for comebacks, provided we frame them correctly.

In essence, emotional resilience is about understanding that we hold the pen to our life story. By consciously choosing to write narratives of strength, hope, and growth, we not only overcome adversities but emerge from them stronger, wiser, and more empowered.

Finding Solace in Supportive Communities

A popular African proverb says, "It takes a village to raise a child." In the broader perspective of life, this adage stands true for adults as well. Our emotional well-being is often influenced by the communities and people surrounding us. In times of crisis, especially when the emotional terrain seems unbearable, a supportive community acts as a haven of understanding, comfort, and strength.

The scam experience led me down a path of isolation initially. There was shame, guilt, and a myriad of overwhelming emotions. But retreating into a shell was not the solution. Slowly, I began reaching out, first to close family members, then to friends, and eventually to communities that resonated with my struggles.

Support groups, both online and offline, were a revelation. Interacting with individuals who had endured similar hardships provided a sense of camaraderie. They were testimonies to the fact that recovery and healing were attainable. Their stories of triumph over adversity, their shared experiences, and the collective wisdom of such groups gave me hope during my darkest hours.

Church communities were another anchor. The congregation wasn't just about shared faith; it was also about shared humanity. Whether it was a kind word, a prayer, or just the comforting silence of understanding, the church community provided a sense of belonging. It was a gentle reminder that even amidst the storm, there was a higher force guiding and watching over me.

Reconnecting with old friends also played a significant role. These were individuals who knew me beyond my present circumstances. They remembered my strengths, passions, and aspirations. Their faith in me, and the cherished shared memories, became the balm to my wounded spirit.

It is also worth noting the importance of diversifying one's support community. Different groups offer different perspectives and forms of support. While some may provide emotional solace, others might offer practical solutions. The key is to recognize what you need and seek out those who can best provide it.

In essence, supportive communities are mirrors reflecting our inner strength and potential, especially when our vision becomes clouded by overwhelming emotions. They hold us, lift us, and walk beside us, ensuring that we never tread the path of recovery alone.

Celebrating Emotional Milestones

As with any journey, the path to emotional resilience is dotted with milestones. These aren't just markers of distance covered but of growth, understanding, and healing. Recognizing and celebrating these milestones is crucial because it serves as an illustration of our progress and encourages continued momentum.

Every small victory on my path of recovery was a milestone: the first time I confronted my emotions instead of suppressing them, the first time I reached out for support, the first time I forgave myself for the financial misstep. Each of these were significant achievements.

Journaling was instrumental in tracking these milestones. Reflecting upon my emotions, actions, and reactions daily provided a clear view of my emotional growth over time. It also allowed me to recognize patterns and anticipate potential triggers or setbacks.

But more than just recognizing these milestones, celebrating them was equally important. Celebrations could be as simple as taking a day off to indulge in a cherished activity, sharing the achievement with a loved one, or even just acknowledging it with a quiet moment of gratitude. Each celebration reinforced positivity, motivation, and the will to continue forward.

Another crucial aspect is sharing these milestones with supportive communities. Doing so not only amplifies the joy but also serves to inspire and uplift others on similar paths. My journey and its successes, when shared, became a source of encouragement for many who were just starting their recovery or were doing it.

Lastly, while celebrating achievements, it's also vital to prepare for the road ahead. Each milestone, while a marker of progress, is also a precursor to the next phase of growth. Being cognizant of this fact ensures that the journey of emotional resilience is ongoing, dynamic, and ever evolving.

In conclusion, emotional milestones aren't just markers of the distance covered. They are heartwarming reminders of our strength, our capacity to heal, and our innate ability to rise above adversities. By recognizing and celebrating them, we not only honor our journey but also pave the way for continued growth, healing, and transformation.

CHAPTER 12

STRATEGIES FOR SELF-EMPOWERMENT

"Act as if what you do makes a difference. It does."

— William James

Affirmations and Visualization Techniques

In the challenging terrains of life, it's easy to feel lost, insecure, and disempowered. One of the most potent tools we possess to counter this dissonance lies in the realm of our mind: affirmations and visualization techniques.

Affirmations are powerful, positive statements that challenge and control negative thoughts or self-doubt and condition the subconscious mind to believe certain things. They aren't simply exercises in "thinking positive," but are profound acknowledgments of one's potential, worth, and abilities. Consider this: every time you repeat an affirmation like, "I am capable of overcoming any obstacle," you're not just trying to negate the negatives but are actively wiring your brain to see challenges as surmountable.

Visualization, on the other hand, is a technique of mentally simulating a desired outcome or process. It's like rehearsing life in your mind's eye. Want to get out of debt? Visualize yourself methodically paying off each debt, experiencing the joy of each bill marked as 'paid,' and feeling the relief when you're finally debt-free. The brain often struggles to differentiate between what's vividly imagined and what's real. Hence, frequent visualizations can condition the brain to behave in a way that aligns with the visualized scenarios.

Both affirmations and visualization can be synergized. For instance, while affirming your financial competence, visualize a clear scene of you managing your finances with prowess. This duality creates a multi-sensory experience, amplifying the impact. However, these tools demand consistency. They aren't just one-time rituals but daily practices that, over time, reshape the mind's patterns, turning self-doubt into confidence and challenges into opportunities.

Setting and Enforcing Healthy Boundaries

In the pursuit of self-empowerment, it's not just about fueling inner strength but also about safeguarding that strength. This is where setting and enforcing healthy boundaries come into play.

Boundaries are personal rules or limits we set for ourselves to ensure our well-being and maintain our integrity. They delineate where our limits are and prevent others from overstepping or taking advantage of our generosity. For someone who's naturally giving, like a mother who's been through thick and thin, it's crucial to recognize that setting boundaries isn't selfish. It's a necessary act of self-preservation.

Imagine you're a vessel filled with water. Every time someone needs water, you give a little. Over time, without boundaries, you'd be emptied. However, setting a boundary is similar to having a tap with a control knob. You can give water when needed, but also ensure you never run dry. This isn't just about conserving; it's about ensuring you always have something to give.

Initiating boundaries can be challenging, especially for those conditioned to be perennial givers. It might feel like you're turning your back on those in need. But it's essential to understand that by setting limits, you're not diminishing your love or support; you're simply defining how you can offer it without harming yourself.

Enforcing boundaries can be equally challenging. It requires firmness, clarity, and consistency. When someone tries to cross a boundary, it's imperative to communicate calmly yet firmly, ensuring they understand your stance. With time, as these boundaries become evident, those around you will begin to recognize and respect them.

In the end, setting and enforcing healthy boundaries is not about building walls but about planting fences with gates. It's about controlling the inflow and outflow, ensuring that in the midst of giving, you don't lose yourself. It's a pivotal strategy in the journey towards genuine self-empowerment.

In my life, one glaring pattern emerged: the lack of boundaries. For as long as I could remember, I championed the role of the giver, extending my hand to anyone in need. While this might sound like a noble trait, it came with its pitfalls. My propensity to give knew no limits, and because I seldom received, I found myself emotionally, physically, and even financially depleted.

From early on, I unknowingly erected a sign that told the world, "It's okay to tread on my territory," and tread they did. It was this absence of barriers that became my Achilles' heel. While I had a heart that overflowed with love and kindness, I did not equip myself with the protective walls needed to shield that heart from exploitation. My belief in the inherent goodness of people overshadowed the essential self-love and self-respect that are vital for personal well-being.

The belief that I was undeserving of the bounties life had to offer plagued me. This self-deprecating mindset made me an easy target for those who sensed my vulnerabilities. It was as if they had a sixth sense for detecting individuals like me. It's a painful realization, but my story, particularly with the scammer, reflects this very sentiment. He, like many before him, identified my lack of boundaries. They saw the spaces where protective walls should have stood and instead found open gates, welcoming them in.

My emotions became the strings by which others could puppeteer me. The scammer was no exception. He danced his way around my insecurities, manipulating situations to his advantage. While he was a pronounced example, there were countless others who sought my help, time, resources, and emotions, regardless of the personal toll it took on me. Each time I said "yes" when every fiber of my being screamed "no," I handed over a piece of my peace.

This is not to say that generosity or kindness is flawed. Quite the opposite. These are virtues the world desperately needs. However, like a priceless artifact in a museum, they need to be encased in protective boundaries, ensuring they are neither misused nor taken for granted.

Looking back on this chapter of my life, I recognize that my struggles stemmed from an inherent lack of self-value. I was caught in a tumultuous storm, unable to anchor myself because I didn't deem myself worthy of the protection an anchor provides. However, it's never too late to learn and grow. Life handed me a lesson, albeit a painful one, on the importance of establishing boundaries. To value oneself is to understand that while giving is commendable, it must be balanced with receiving, protecting one's peace, and, above all, loving oneself unabashedly.

For those reading my story, understand this: your worth is immeasurable. Guard your heart, your peace, and your self-respect with the fierceness of a lion. While it's beautiful to have a heart that gives, it's equally essential to have boundaries that protect. Let my journey be a testament to the importance of finding that balance.

Continuous Learning and Growth

In the vast, ever-changing landscape of life, there's one compass that consistently points us in the direction of enrichment and empowerment: continuous learning and growth.

Continuous learning isn't limited to the acquisition of new knowledge or skills. It's an ongoing process of refining our perspectives, challenging our beliefs, and deepening our understanding of ourselves and the world around us. This holistic approach to learning serves as a reminder that every experience, be it positive or negative, holds a lesson. Like the protagonist of our story, who faced severe financial setbacks and emotional trials, every pitfall or hurdle encountered is an invitation to learn, adapt, and rise stronger.

However, this growth mindset requires nurturing. Embracing continuous learning means staying curious, being open to feedback, and seeking opportunities to stretch beyond our comfort zones. It might be in the form of reading books, attending workshops, or engaging in reflective practices. But at its core, it's about recognizing that growth isn't a destination but a journey. The path may sometimes be steep or rocky, but the vistas it opens up, the insights gained, and the empowerment it offers make every step worth it.

Moreover, this ongoing journey of learning offers something invaluable: adaptability. In a world that's in a constant state of flux, the ability to learn and adapt becomes not just a skill but a survival trait. It ensures we're not left behind, that we continue to evolve in tandem with our environment. And in doing so, we equip ourselves with the tools not just to survive but to thrive.

Celebrating Personal Power

There's a quiet strength, a reservoir of power, that resides within each of us. It's the force that fuels our spirit during the most challenging times, the spark that ignites our resilience, and the voice that whispers, "You can do it," when the world screams otherwise. This is our personal power, and it deserves to be celebrated.

Personal power isn't about domination or imposing one's will on others. It's about recognizing our inherent worth, our capabilities, and the unique gifts we bring to the table. It's about understanding that no matter the trials we face or the mistakes we make, our essence remains untarnished. We hold within us the power to reinvent, rebuild, and rise.

Celebrating personal power is an act of acknowledging our journey, our struggles, and our victories. It's a tribute to every time we chose to stand up after a fall, every moment we decided to push forward despite the odds. But more than that, it's a recognition of our autonomy. The realization that we have the agency to shape our destiny, make choices, and influence outcomes.

But how do we celebrate this power?

> **Firstly**, by owning our story. Every chapter, every line, every twist in the tale. By understanding that our experiences, both good and bad, have contributed to the person we've become.
>
> **Secondly**, by being kind to ourselves, offering ourselves the same compassion and understanding we'd extend to a dear friend.
>
> **And lastly**, by using this power for good, channeling it not just to uplift our spirits but also to make a positive impact in the lives of those around us.

In essence, celebrating personal power is about basking in the light of our authentic selves, letting that light shine brightly, and using it as an example for others, too. It's a powerful demonstration of the incredible potential that resides within, waiting to be tapped, cherished, and revered.

CHAPTER 13

EMBRACING GRIEF, LOSS, AND SERENDIPITY

> *"In the midst of winter, I found there was, within me, an invincible summer."*
>
> — Albert Camus

Navigating Grief and Loss

Grief and loss are experiences so profound, so universal, that they tie humanity together in an intricate web of shared pain and healing. The shadows they cast are undeniably dark, but within them lie profound lessons, moments of clarity, and the chance for personal growth.

Drawing from my own narrative, I've tasted the bitterness of loss more times than I'd care to recall. There were moments, whether due to personal betrayals, business failures, or the devastating scam ordeal, where I felt like a ship lost in the fog. But even in those darkest times, I learned that there's a certain power in vulnerability and even more in the journey to find meaning amidst the chaos.

I remember the first time grief hit me like a tidal wave, washing away the vibrant colors of my world. It came when I lost my father in a tragic plane crash. This profound loss was not just a singular event of sadness; it was a complex tapestry of emotions—anger, confusion, denial, and fleeting moments of acceptance. Grief, I learned, was not linear. It ebbed and flowed, sometimes receding and at other times crashing down with unexpected ferocity.

As I navigated through life, this tidal wave of grief revisited me, albeit in different forms. The loss of my grandmother and, later, my beloved mother left a void no words could fill. These losses, like landmarks of my journey, brought a deep sense of longing and an acute awareness of life's fragility. Each loss etched its own story of pain and tenacity within me.

Finding Meaning in the Darkness

Journeying through grief is an intensely personal experience, yet it also unfolds universal truths. The scam ordeal, a different kind of loss, not only stripped me of my financial security but also robbed me of trust and shook my self-worth to its core. In this darkness, however, I discovered glimmers of light. Each of these ordeals, as heartbreaking as they were, propelled me to reevaluate what truly mattered. They urged me to rediscover my strengths and to acknowledge the genuine, unwavering supports in my life.

Grief, I realized, often acts like a magnifying glass, accentuating aspects of our lives that we might have previously overlooked. The simple joys, the silent supporters, the resilience hidden deep within us—they all come into sharp focus against the backdrop of loss. These lessons, these silver linings, became evident as I navigated my way through the profound losses of my father, grandmother, mother, and the emotional aftermath of the scam.

In embracing these experiences of loss, I learned to see them not just as moments of pain but as opportunities for profound personal growth and a deeper understanding of the intricate dance of life's highs and lows.

Lessons for the Journey Ahead

Embrace Your Emotions: Don't shy away from your feelings, no matter how tumultuous they may be. Let yourself feel, process, and gradually heal. Each emotion is a step on the ladder to recovery.

Seek Support: Remember, even in your loneliest moments, you're not alone. Reach out, whether to loved ones, professional therapists, or support groups. Sharing eases the burden and often brings new perspectives.

Reframe and Refocus: This is a lesson borrowed from Bob's teachings. Reframing isn't about denying the pain but about finding a new way to look at it. Maybe it's seeing a loss as a redirection or a betrayal as a lesson in self-worth.

Seek Purpose: When enveloped in grief, it's easy to lose sight of purpose. But sometimes, it's within the depths of loss that we find our most profound calling. For me, every setback was a setup for a stronger comeback.

Celebrate Memories: The pain of loss is undeniable, but so are the memories that preceded it. Celebrate them. Cherish them. Let them be a source of warmth and comfort.

Grief and loss are, tragically, an inevitable part of the human experience. But they're also transformative. Through the pain, through the tears, there's an opportunity for growth, learning, and renewal. My journey, with its peaks and valleys, is a testament to the strength of the human spirit and the enduring quest for meaning.

To every reader navigating their storm of grief, remember that the sun, however distant it might seem now, will shine again. Your pain, while profound, is also a bridge to deeper understanding, compassion, and a renewed zest for life. Embrace the journey, with all its lessons and trials, and know that in this shared voyage of life, you're never truly alone.

Moments of Serendipity

Life has a peculiar way of serving surprises. Sometimes, the most unexpected events, the ones that catch you off guard, pave the way for profound realizations and unforeseen joyous outcomes. These are our moments of serendipity—when the Universe conspires to give us something we never knew we needed. Let's dive into two personal tales of serendipity and their profound impact.

1. From Bankruptcy to Financial Enlightenment

The anguish of a relationship breakdown is a tumultuous storm, but in this tempest, I found myself facing an even darker cloud: bankruptcy. As heartrending as it was, this phase forced me to look my vulnerabilities square in the eye. It wasn't just about lost love; it was also about lost financial security.

The days that followed were grim. Bankruptcy has a way of tainting your self-worth. But then, amidst the chaos, something incredible happened. Instead of succumbing to despair, I chose to learn, grow, and build from scratch. My financial pitfall transformed into a classroom.

Instead of seeing bankruptcy as a failure, I began to see it as a lesson in financial management. With determination, I immersed myself in understanding money, savings, and investments. The result? Not only did I recover from bankruptcy, but I also became adept at handling personal finances, ensuring I'd never fall into a debt trap again. What seemed like a terrible stroke of misfortune turned out to be a blessing in disguise—a serendipitous event that propelled me towards financial wisdom.

2. From Samoan Shores to Australian Dreams

At fifteen, leaving Samoa was more than just a relocation; it was leaving a part of my soul behind. Friends, familiar sights, sounds, the culture I loved, all were to be traded for an alien land. Australia beckoned, and with a heavy heart, I stepped onto its soil, unable to communicate or integrate seamlessly because of the language barrier.

The initial days in Australia were challenging. The cultural differences were vast, and not speaking English made integration seem almost impossible. Every day presented a challenge, from understanding lessons at school to simply making friends.

But as days turned to weeks and weeks to months, the unexpected began to unfold. With every challenge I faced, there was an opportunity to grow. The effort to learn English led me not only to communicate but to excel in my studies. The struggle to fit in taught me to find common ground amidst diversity.

Finishing school was a triumph, an indication of overcoming initial adversities. The friendships forged became lifelong bonds, proving that relationships are built on understanding and mutual respect, not just shared cultural backgrounds. And the appreciation for Australia grew, not as a replacement but as an addition to my Samoan heritage. The journey, which started with uncertainty, culminated in achieving higher education and tasting success in a land once foreign.

These early challenges in Australia were not mere obstacles; they were serendipitous events steering me towards personal growth, resilience, and success.

A Universal Truth

Serendipity is not just about happy accidents; it's about perspective. It's about viewing every challenge, setback, or unexpected event as an opportunity waiting to be seized. In both stories, what seemed like daunting adversities at first glance turned out to be pivotal moments leading to personal growth and success.

Life is peppered with such moments. All we need is the lens to recognize them and the spirit to embrace them. Remember: sometimes, the Universe takes away what we think we want to give us what we truly need. Embrace every twist, every turn, and trust that often, the most unexpected routes lead to the most beautiful destinations.

Life is unpredictable, but it's these serendipitous moments that add color, teach lessons, and offer a deeper understanding of ourselves and the world around us. They remind us that even in uncertainty, there's always a silver lining.

CHAPTER 14

NURTURING SPIRITUAL GROWTH

*"The soul always knows what to do to heal itself.
The challenge is to silence the mind."*

— Caroline Myss

Daily Spiritual Practices for Well-being

In an age where screens flash, notifications ping, and life rushes past us, pausing to nourish our spiritual essence becomes our compass. Our spirituality isn't just a lofty idea; it's the bridge connecting us to the vast Universe, our higher self, and the Divine in ways that words often fail to capture. This bond is a lighthouse, guiding and giving us the strength to navigate the storms of life.

Engaging in daily spiritual practices isn't merely a ritual; it's a commitment to our soul. Just as we feed our body to fuel our physical journey, our spirit, too, needs sustenance to enlighten our path. It is this spiritual nutrition that infuses life with depth, purpose, and meaning.

During my personal trials and tribulations, I've found an incredible reservoir of strength in my spiritual routines. Such practices not only anchor us but also illuminate our journey, reminding us of the larger picture and our role within it.

Meditation, a timeless spiritual tool, illustrates the wonders of inner reflection. It's not merely about sitting quietly; it's a voyage inward. Even dedicating just a few moments each day to meditation can transform our minds, gifting us clarity, tranquility, and a heart that resonates with the Universe's rhythm.

Similarly, mindfulness, the art of being truly present, is like a soft whisper in our ear, reminding us to cherish each heartbeat, each breath. In our hectic lives, where time seems to slip through our fingers, embracing every moment becomes a radical act. Whether it's savoring the warmth of a morning cup of tea or basking in the gratitude of simply being alive, mindfulness reconnects us to the miracle of existence.

But there's another spiritual practice that has been my rock: prayer. The power of prayer transcends mere words. It's a conversation with God, an intimate dialogue with the Divine. When we pray, we pour our hopes, dreams, fears, and gratitude into the cosmos, forging a connection that's unbreakable. In moments of despair, when the weight of the world felt too heavy, it was my prayers that uplifted me, reassuring me that I was never alone in my journey.

Alongside these, immersing oneself in spiritual texts or the rhythmic flow of yoga can serve as daily reminders of the vastness of our existence and the interconnectedness of all beings. They become our spiritual touchpoints, anchoring us when the tides get rough and celebrating with us in moments of joy.

In essence, our spiritual practices are more than mere routines; they're lifelines, channels that constantly remind us of our purpose, our connection, and the boundless love and strength that resides within each of us. They teach us, guide us, and, most importantly, help us see the light even on the darkest nights.

The Joy of Spiritual Retreats

While daily spiritual practices provide consistent sustenance for the soul, occasionally, we need to dive deeper. This is where spiritual retreats and journeys come into play. They serve as intensive periods of reflection, growth, and transformation, allowing for a deeper dive into one's spiritual self than daily rituals might provide.

Retreats are often set in serene environments, away from the hustle and bustle of urban life. This physical detachment from the mundane allows for an immersive spiritual experience. Whether it's a silent retreat in the woods, a meditation camp in the mountains, or a pilgrimage to a holy site, the very act of setting aside time and space for spiritual growth is transformative.

The essence of such journeys lies not just in their destinations but in the experiences they foster. Disconnecting from daily routines, from the ever-present pull of digital devices, and spending time in reflection and spiritual practice can bring about profound inner shifts.

It's not uncommon to hear of epiphanies or life-altering realizations during such retreats. The silence and peace allow for deep introspection, often leading to a clearer understanding and direction in life. Furthermore, these retreats often provide the opportunity to connect with like-minded individuals, creating a sense of community and shared purpose.

There's also a unique joy in undertaking spiritual journeys. Whether it's walking the Camino de Santiago in Spain, meditating in an ashram in India, or joining a Native American vision quest, these journeys can be deeply personal and transformative. The challenges faced, the insights gained, and the sheer joy of spiritual exploration make these experiences invaluable.

In conclusion, while our daily spiritual practices anchor us, the depth and breadth of spiritual retreats and journeys provide the intensive nourishment our souls occasionally need. Both are crucial in the journey of spiritual growth, each complementing the other in a dance of depth and consistency.

Deepening Connections with the Divine

The relationship with the Divine, however one perceives it—whether as God, the Universe, Higher Power, or another sacred force—is an intimate journey of the spirit. It is as unique as one's fingerprint and is shaped by personal experiences, beliefs, and understandings.

As the relationship deepens, it's akin to peeling back the layers of an onion; each layer brings forth a new revelation, a new understanding, and a new connection. This intimacy, however, isn't achieved overnight. It requires effort, introspection, and, often, a deliberate choice to pursue this sacred connection amidst the cacophony of life.

Many seekers embark on this journey by choosing dedicated moments of silence and solitude. It is in the stillness that one often hears the gentle whispers of the Divine. The sacred is not necessarily in grand gestures but often in the subtle, almost silent moments: the sudden rustle of leaves, the soft gurgling of a brook, or the stillness of a predawn morning.

Sacred texts, regardless of religious orientation, often offer a reservoir of wisdom and insight. Delving into these reservoirs, not just as literature but as living testaments of Divine wisdom, allows for a richer understanding of the Divine's nature. It's like a dialogue, where one finds answers to life's questions, comfort in moments of despair, and guidance in times of uncertainty.

Furthermore, practicing unconditional love and kindness often leads to a deepened connection with the Divine. Recognizing the Divine spark in every individual and treating each life as a sacred manifestation of the higher power is transformative. The act of love, in its purest form, becomes both a path to and a reflection of the Divine.

Sharing Spiritual Gifts and Insights

Just as a lamp can light another without diminishing its own flame, sharing one's spiritual insights and gifts frequently enriches one's own spiritual journey. The act of sharing isn't just about imparting knowledge or wisdom; it's about creating connections, fostering community, and nurturing a collective consciousness.

There is an indescribable joy in sharing, especially when it comes to spiritual insights. It's not about preaching or converting; it's about holding space for others to experience the same light that has illuminated one's own path. When spiritual insights are shared, they resonate, creating ripples of understanding and awareness that can touch countless lives.

Moreover, sharing isn't limited to verbal communication. One can share spiritual gifts through acts of kindness, creating art, writing, or simply being present for someone. It's in these acts that one truly embodies the spiritual lessons they've garnered, allowing others to witness and partake in the Divine dance.

As one grows spiritually, the realization dawns that the journey is not solitary. We are intricately connected in this web of life, and every insight, every moment of enlightenment, is not just personal but universal. In sharing, one recognizes this interconnectedness, understanding that everyone's growth contributes to the collective evolution.

Furthermore, sharing fosters a sense of community. When individuals come together to share spiritual insights, it creates a safe space for exploration, questioning, and understanding. It's a communion of souls, each bringing their unique perspectives and insights, contributing to a richer, more diverse understanding of the Divine and the human experience.

In conclusion, the act of deepening one's connection with the Divine is an inward journey, while sharing spiritual gifts and insights is the outward expression of this journey. Both are integral to spiritual growth. The former nurtures the soul, while the latter allows the soul to blossom, spreading its fragrance to the world around.

CHAPTER 15

ASCENDING TO NEW HEIGHTS

"The best view comes after the hardest climb."

— Unknown

Recognizing Life's Cyclical Nature

Life is a symphony of cycles: seasons that flow into one another, echoing the innate rhythm of existence. As we witness the grandeur of nature, we are reminded that the trees shed their leaves only to welcome new ones, the tide ebbs only to flow again, and the sun sets only to rise once more. Such is the cyclical nature of life, a constant reminder that every ending paves the way for a new beginning.

Embracing the cyclical nature of life is pivotal to personal growth and understanding. Just as a caterpillar undergoes transformation to emerge as a butterfly, our lives, too, are punctuated by periods of struggle that lead to times of renewal. By acknowledging these cycles, we find solace in the idea that difficult phases are not permanent; they're merely precursors to times of rejuvenation and rebirth.

Moreover, these cycles serve as teaching moments. Each phase offers unique lessons, molding us into stronger, wiser beings. Our challenges and hardships are, in essence, our most significant teachers. They teach us resilience, patience, and the transformative power of perseverance.

A crucial realization is that while we might not always control external circumstances, we can control our reactions. By recognizing the cyclical nature of life, we can approach challenges with a mindset of growth. Instead of being overwhelmed by the weight of difficulties, we can see them as necessary phases leading us to our next period of prosperity and growth.

Another aspect of these cycles is the understanding of impermanence. Nothing remains static. This knowledge is a comforting reminder during challenging times that "this too shall pass." Conversely, during moments of joy, it serves as a nudge to cherish and be grateful, for these moments are fleeting.

In essence, recognizing life's cyclical nature is a journey of embracing change, understanding impermanence, and growing through every phase. It's about learning to dance in the rain, knowing that the sun will shine again, and understanding that every sunset is a promise of a new dawn.

Welcoming New Beginnings After Endings

Every ending is a new beginning in disguise. Whether it's the end of a relationship, a job, or a phase in our life, each ending carries with it the seed of a fresh start. Yet, our perception often blinds us to this reality. We mourn the loss, the change, and the unfamiliarity of it all. But beneath this veil of uncertainty lies a realm of possibilities, just waiting to be explored.

The concept of "endings" is deeply embedded in our psyche as something negative. We resist change, hold on to memories, and often remain trapped in the past. However, this resistance hinders our growth. Only when we embrace the idea of new beginnings do we unlock our potential and step into a new chapter of our lives.

Welcoming new beginnings requires a shift in mindset. Instead of seeing endings as losses, I can choose to view them as opportunities. Every ending is a lesson, an experience that has shaped me. And as one door closes, countless others await to be opened.

Starting anew is a chance to redefine myself. It's an invitation to revisit my goals, aspirations, and the path I wish to walk. Each new beginning offers a blank canvas, allowing me to paint my journey as I envision.

Furthermore, new beginnings often come with a renewed sense of purpose and energy. The freshness of starting over, the excitement of the unknown, and the thrill of exploration can be incredibly invigorating. It propels us forward, urging us to step out of our comfort zones and embrace the myriad of opportunities that life presents.

However, welcoming new beginnings also necessitates letting go. Letting go of past regrets, of memories that no longer serve us, and of any baggage that weighs us down. It's about making peace with the past, cherishing the memories but not allowing them to tether us.

In conclusion, life is a series of chapters, each with its own set of endings and beginnings. By recognizing life's cyclical nature and welcoming the fresh starts that come our way, we set ourselves on a path of continual growth, evolution, and ascension. It's a tribute to the human spirit's tenacity and our innate ability to rise, time and time again, ascending to newer heights.

Paving the Path for Others

In our journey of personal growth and ascension, we often find ourselves standing on the shoulders of giants—those who came before us, showing us the way, making our paths clearer and more manageable. As we ascend to new heights in our own lives, there arises a profound responsibility, almost a rite of passage: to become the guiding force for others, to pave their paths just as ours were laid before us.

History is replete with luminaries who, after achieving their dreams, dedicated their lives to ensuring others could reach similar pinnacles. These torchbearers recognized that true success isn't just about personal achievements; it's about enabling others to realize their potential.

Paving the path for others is an endeavor of profound significance. It's about mentorship, about sharing acquired wisdom, experiences, and insights. It's about recognizing potential in others, often before they see it in themselves, and nurturing it. Every time we help another person move forward, every time we inspire hope or serve as a pillar of support, we contribute to a chain of positive change that can span generations.

This act of guiding isn't just limited to grand gestures. It's in the daily acts of kindness, the words of encouragement, the listening ear, and the shared insights. It's in the workshops we conduct, the books we write, and the stories we share. Each of these actions holds the potential to inspire, motivate, and pave the way for someone else.

Furthermore, as we help others rise, our own understanding deepens, and our perspectives broaden. In teaching, we learn. In giving, we receive. The act of guiding others, in many ways, becomes a twofold journey of growth.

In essence, paving the path for others is a celebration of our shared humanity. It depicts the interconnectedness of our journeys. While each person's path is unique, the challenges, emotions, and aspirations are often universally shared. Recognizing this shared journey and stepping up to guide others is perhaps one of the most fulfilling endeavors one can undertake.

A Lifelong Commitment to the Climb

Life, with its myriad challenges, joys, sorrows, and triumphs, is akin to a mountain climb. It presents steep slopes, unexpected terrains, breathtaking views, and moments that test our stamina and resolve. But as any seasoned climber would attest, the thrill lies not just in reaching the peak, but in the climb itself.

A lifelong commitment to the climb means embracing the journey of life with all its nuances. It's about understanding that life isn't a destination but a continuous journey of growth, learning, and evolution. Each phase, each challenge, each joy is a part of this endless ascent, and the beauty lies in savoring each step.

The commitment to this climb means recognizing that there will be times of struggle, times when the peak seems unreachable. But it's in these moments of doubt that our true strength emerges. By staying committed, we harness our inner resilience, draw from our past experiences, and keep pushing forward.

However, this commitment isn't just about perseverance. It's also about adaptability and flexibility. Just as a climber must adapt to changing weather conditions, we, too, must learn to navigate the unpredictable terrains of life. It's about knowing when to push forward, when to pause and rest, and when to seek an alternate route.

Furthermore, a lifelong commitment to the climb is also a commitment to self-awareness and introspection. With each step, we gain a deeper understanding of ourselves—our strengths, our vulnerabilities, our passions, and our fears. This self-awareness becomes our compass, guiding us and ensuring we stay true to our path.

In addition, this commitment also extends to the community around us. It's about lifting others as we rise, celebrating collective successes, and facing challenges together. It's about understanding that while the climb is personal, the journey is shared.

In conclusion, a lifelong commitment to the climb is a celebration of life in its entirety. It's an acknowledgment of the highs and lows, the joys and sorrows, and the lessons each phase brings. By committing to this journey, we not only embrace our own growth but also contribute to the collective ascent of those around us. Life's climb is arduous, unpredictable, and profoundly beautiful, and our commitment to it makes the journey truly worthwhile.

CHAPTER 16

REFLECTIONS AND REVELATIONS

> *"In the dance of life, every stumble leads to a new step; it's our heart's rhythm that turns setbacks into symphonies."*
>
> — Naise Silapa

My Reflections

Life's kinda like hiking a big ol' mountain, isn't it? There are those mega high points, where you feel on top of the world, and then those deep, dark valleys that make you question why you even started climbing in the first place. But looking back at those mud-covered boots and all the zigzags on our trail? Man, it's not just about that epic view from the summit. It's about the slips, the breaks, the "Oops, should've taken that turn," and those leaps of faith I took every single day.

You know that saying, "It's not about the destination, but the journey"? This whole book? It's a shout-out to that. It's a diary of not just the miles walked but the lessons learned, the toughness earned, and the whole personal makeover I went through.

Each story, feeling, and surprise twist? That's me, climbing my personal life ladder, pushing my limits, and seeing just how far I can really go.

Let's be real—this climb was a wild ride. Like climbing Everest without a map kind of wild. The burnouts, the "I'm done with this" moments? Totally felt those. But aren't those tricky paths the ones that really show us what we're made of? And that scam saga? It wasn't just a plot twist. It was our reality check. It pushed all the buttons, tested all my defenses, and even brought out some ghosts I didn't know I had. But on the flip side? Hello, newfound strength! Through all the lows and "Oh no's," I found a version of myself that was tougher, kinder, and even danced better to life's crazy beats.

Life's Hidden Lessons and Our Cheer Squad

Looking back, all those bumps, detours, and even that scam were sort of like hidden life tutorials. They taught me to draw lines, value myself, and realize that bouncing back is kinda my superpower. Every tiny twist? It's all part of this big, beautiful, messy art piece I call life.

Can't forget my backstage crew, though—my beloved mother, sister, my children, family, friends, and even those happy accidents (thank you, Universe!). They were the push when I felt stuck, the background score that made my journey feel like a blockbuster movie. With them, every step felt like a dance move, turning the whole climb into something epic.

So, here's to the climb. To every scratch, tear, and that one memory that makes us both laugh and cringe. They aren't just old stories gathering dust; they're our battle scars, proof that we took on life's game and scored big.

To all you fellow climbers out there, remember, every rough patch is just a page in your life's epic novel. They lead to chapters that are even more wild, full of hope, surprises, and endless "Whoa, did that just happen?" moments. So, hug your journey tight, celebrate every inch you climb, and always know there's another peak waiting, whispering, "Bet you can't reach me!"

At the heart of it, this climb? It's all about the crazy, unpredictable, glorious ride of life. It's a big high-five to our unbreakable spirit, the dreamers' hearts, and every soul brave enough to trek the unknown with a backpack full of hope and a pocket full of grit.

A Message of Hope and Inspiration for Fellow Travelers

You ever think of life as one big, unpredictable road trip? Some days, you're cruising along scenic routes, sunroof open, wind in your hair. On others, you're stuck in a thunderstorm with a flat tire, no map, and a dying phone. But guess what? Even during those torrential downpours, there's this tiny light up ahead, a beacon of hope. And that's what I want to share with you today: a flashlight for your journey, to help you see beyond the bends.

Remember those shadows that sometimes loom large, making everything seem so dark and daunting? They're just temporary clouds blocking out your sun. Adversities, challenges, the whole shebang—they're not here to tie you down but to set you up for something even better. Believe me, my life's been a roller-coaster, but each drop, each twist, each loop showed me the fire I had inside.

Your scars? Those aren't badges of defeat. Nope. They're medals of honor. Battle scars from life's great wars. They tell stories of resilience, of struggles faced head-on, and of all those dragons you've slain on your way. My own scars have shown me just how much grit, guts, and gumption I've got.

Feeling alone? Trust me, even when things seem bleak and the nights never-ending, there are stars up above, just waiting for you to look up. This journey isn't about getting from Point A to B. It's about the laughs, the tears, the memories, the stories, the people you meet, and all the love you gather. When I was knee-deep in my own mess, it was the collective human experience that gave me a lifeline.

Let's talk dreams. Dream BIG. Go beyond your fears, ignore the naysayers, and just fly. After falling for a scam once, it was my dreams that were my compass, turning my mess into a message.

Looking for a muse? Hit pause. Take a moment. The Universe is a chatterbox if you know how to listen. The rustling leaves? They're whispering secrets of resilience. The slow streams? They're telling tales of patience. Every sunrise? That's nature's lesson on fresh starts.

Bridges, Bonds, and the Beauty of the Now

On this wild ride called life, wear your kindness like armor and wield empathy like a sword. Show some love to others, and don't forget to pamper your own soul. Each misstep, every tear, it's all part of this grand adventure. With a sprinkle of kindness and a dash of empathy, the healing's quicker and the journey richer.

Amongst all the places you'll go, the best spots? They aren't on any map. They're those magical moments—a laugh shared, an understanding smile, or a warm embrace. They're the true milestones, the memories you'll cherish forever.

So, to all you wanderers, explorers, and dreamers, here's a high-five from a fellow traveler. Sure, the path's often rocky and the mountains steep, but we've got that unyielding spirit, an ironclad resolve, and a world of possibilities ahead. Let's take this journey together, spreading hope and lighting up each other's paths. And in this combined glow, we'll find our real destination. Onward, fellow traveler! Let's make this journey count. ✹

CHAPTER 17

CHARTING A CLEAR COURSE TO SUCCESS

"The best way to predict your future is to create it."
— Peter Drucker

Understanding the Importance of Direction

Every great journey begins with a clear destination in mind. Just as a captain charts a course before setting sail, we too must define our life's direction. This clarity isn't just about setting goals; it's about understanding our deepest values and aspirations. It's about aligning our dreams with our actions.

In the vast expanse of the Pacific, tiny islands like Samoa serve as guiding stars for navigators. Similarly, in life, having a clear sense of direction is paramount. As I navigated the challenges of my early life, from the trauma of loss to facing the adversities of family turmoil, I realized that having a direction was more than just a goal; it was my North Star. A sense of direction isn't just about knowing where you're going; it's about understanding why that destination matters.

Maxwell Maltz emphasizes this beautifully in *Psycho-Cybernetics*. He presents the idea that our brains operate much like a missile. A missile needs a target, and without it, it's merely wandering aimlessly. The same applies to our lives. Without a sense of direction, we are susceptible to the winds of circumstance, easily swayed off course.

Reflecting upon my days in Samoa, I remember looking after my siblings and cousins, taking on responsibilities most kids my age wouldn't dream of. There were times I felt lost, almost drifting in the vastness of responsibilities. But what kept me going? A direction, a hope that things would change, and the understanding that I had a role to play in that change.

Defining Your Personal North Star

Everyone's sense of direction, their personal North Star, is unique. For some, it might be achieving a particular career milestone; for others, it might be ensuring the well-being and happiness of their family. As I journeyed through life, my North Star was a blend of ensuring my family's happiness and personal growth.

Our 'North Star' serves as our guiding light, steering us through life's tumultuous seas. It's a deeply personal journey of discovery, where we reflect on our past experiences, our present circumstances, and our future aspirations. Defining this North Star requires introspection—it's about asking ourselves what truly fulfills us, what legacy we want to leave, and what impact we want to have on the world around us.

One of the crucial lessons I learned from Maxwell Maltz's book *Psycho-Cybernetics* is that our North Star should be a dynamic blend of our aspirations, learnings, and life experiences. The trauma of losing my parentnd the adversities I faced in my family taught me the importance of resilience, love, and patience. These experiences weren't just events; they became foundational pillars upon which I defined my direction.

A sense of direction isn't a passive state of mind; it requires action, continuous realignment, and reflection. It's like being on a journey; the road will have its share of bumps and turns, but what matters is how you navigate through them.

I recall the dread of Fridays in Samoa, days when chaos ensued in my household. But amidst that chaos, I found my direction—safeguarding my younger siblings. That sense of responsibility, although heavy, gave me clarity. Every decision, from hiding to seeking help, was aligned with that direction. Knowing your direction is the first step, but aligning your actions with this direction is what propels you forward. This alignment is about making daily choices that are congruent with your North Star. It's about turning intentions into actions. It could be as simple as dedicating time each day towards a long-term goal or as complex as making significant life changes that better align with your values.

Similarly, when faced with the fear of my health condition, it was my direction—my commitment to self-care and well-being—that finally gave me the courage to get tested. That direction was not just about ensuring my physical well-being but also about emotional and mental resilience.

Maxwell Maltz was right in placing "sense of direction" as the foundational step to success. It's not about just setting a goal; it's about understanding the 'why' behind that goal. It's about aligning our experiences, our aspirations, and our actions towards a meaningful direction. My life's pathway, with its highs and lows, has been a testament to this principle. As we move forward, let's remember: to navigate the vast ocean of life, we need our North Star, our sense of direction.

Cultivating Strength through Direction

Resilience, often regarded as the backbone of success, is not an innate trait but a cultivated attribute. It thrives on the sense of direction we establish in our lives. This topic explores how having a clear direction in life acts as a catalyst for resilience, enabling us to bounce back from setbacks more robustly.

Just as a compass guides a sailor through turbulent waters, our sense of direction serves as our compass through life's storms. It provides us with the resilience to navigate through adversities, knowing that each step, no matter how challenging, is bringing us closer to our destination.

Reflecting on my personal journey, I realize the resilience to recover from the online scam and subsequent challenges was rooted in the clear direction I had set for myself—a direction that stemmed from my deepest values and aspirations. This direction wasn't just a destination but a path laden with lessons, growth, and self-discovery.

In Samoa, the adversities faced within my family and the responsibilities thrust upon me at a young age were stepping stones that built my resilience. They taught me the importance of facing challenges head-on, finding strength in vulnerability, and relentlessly pursuing my goals. This resilience was further tested and fortified during my transition to life in Australia, where cultural and language barriers presented new challenges.

Resilience is also about adaptability—the ability to adjust our sails when the winds change direction. It's about understanding that while our end goal might remain constant, the path to get there can, and often does, change. This adaptability is a crucial component of resilience, allowing us to embrace change, learn from it, and continue moving forward.

To cultivate resilience, one must first define their direction and then steadfastly commit to it, understanding that the journey will be fraught with obstacles. But it is in overcoming these obstacles that resilience is built, and our direction solidified.

In conclusion, resilience and direction go hand in hand. The stronger our sense of direction, the more resilient we become in the face of life's challenges. This resilience not only propels us forward but also enriches our journey with invaluable experiences and lessons.

The Role of Passion in Defining Direction

Passion is the fuel that powers our journey towards our North Star. It ignites our ambition and keeps us motivated even when the road gets tough. This topic delves into how passion plays a pivotal role in defining and sustaining our sense of direction.

In every endeavor, passion gives us the perseverance to continue, even in the face of adversity. It's what turns a vision into reality. For me, the passion for creating a better life for my family and myself was the driving force behind every decision, every challenge faced, and every victory achieved.

From the responsibilities in Samoa to the challenges in Australia, it was my passion for a better future that kept me going. It was this passion that helped me rise above the pain of the scam ordeal and channel my energies into rebuilding my life.

Passion, however, is more than just a strong feeling; it's a deep-seated desire that aligns with our core values and beliefs. It's what makes our direction meaningful and our journey fulfilling. To discover this passion, one must look inward, reflecting on what brings joy, what stirs the soul, and what aligns with one's deeper purpose.

Once identified, this passion becomes the beacon that guides us towards our North Star. It helps us set goals that are not only ambitious, but also deeply satisfying. It ensures that our path is not just a journey towards a destination but an expression of our true selves.

Passion also has a transformative effect. It turns challenges into opportunities for growth, setbacks into lessons, and dreams into realities. It's the difference between merely existing and truly living.

In conclusion, passion is an indispensable element in defining our sense of direction. It breathes life into our goals, infuses joy into our journey, and ensures that our path is as rewarding as the destination itself. With passion as our guide, our journey towards our North Star becomes an exhilarating adventure, full of possibilities and personal fulfillment.

CONCLUSION

*"Life can only be understood backwards;
but it must be lived forwards."*

— Søren Kierkegaard

In this book, we've traveled through many ups and downs together. From the tough times and the scam that knocked me down, to learning how to stand up again with more strength than I knew I had. Every story and lesson shared here is a part of the quest, but it's also for anyone trying to find their way through their own challenges. Events can challenge our core beliefs, identities, and dreams, but through acceptance, we lay the foundation for healing and growth.

We learned about the importance of never giving up, even when things seem impossible. My mom's wisdom, the struggle of being a single parent, and finding a way out of debt taught us about the strength we all carry inside. We talked about taking small steps towards big changes, finding the good in the bad, and seeing money in a new, positive light.

This trip showed us how to believe in ourselves, how to bounce back from tough times, and how to aim for what we really want in life. It's been about more than just getting through; it's about growing, learning, and becoming better. Surrendering control and aligning with God alleviates burdens of anxiety and doubt.

Remember that your path might have twists and turns, but every step is a chance to learn and to climb higher. By harnessing the mind's power, challenges can be reframed as stepping stones to triumph. You're not alone in this climb. With trust, hard work, and a bit of courage, you can reach new heights and see just how far you can go.

Let this book be a guide and a friend for when the road gets rocky. The best views come after the hardest climbs. Keep moving forward, keep aiming high, and believe in your power to overcome anything.

BONUS: MY 12-STEP PATH TO OVERCOMING SETBACKS AND BOUNCING BACK HIGHER

"In every stumble and each misstep, I found a blueprint for rising; a 12-step dance towards resilience, reclaiming my power with every stride."

Step 1. Self-Awareness:

In the labyrinth of life, self-awareness is the compass that points us in the direction of our true selves. It is the first beacon of light that shines brightly when we find ourselves lost in the shadows of setbacks. When a crisis strikes, such as the painful experience of being scammed, the initial wave of emotions can be overpowering. There's a whirlwind of disbelief, anger, and despair that can obscure our understanding of the situation.

Self-awareness is the intentional act of turning inward and acknowledging these emotions without judgment. It is about understanding your personal strengths and weaknesses, recognizing patterns in your behavior, and being attuned to your emotional responses. By being self-aware, you can identify why a particular setback hit so hard. Did it challenge your core values? Did it remind you of past traumas?

Tips & Advice:

Journaling: One of the most effective ways to cultivate self-awareness is to keep a journal. Write down your feelings, thoughts, and reactions to different situations. Over time, you will see patterns emerge.

Mindfulness Meditation: Mindfulness helps you stay rooted in the present. Through regular practice, you'll learn to observe your emotions without getting caught up in them.

Seek Feedback: Sometimes, an external perspective can offer insights into your blind spots. Trusted friends or mentors can provide constructive feedback on your behaviors and reactions.

Set Aside Reflective Time: Dedicate a few minutes each day to introspection. Use this time to think about your actions, decisions, and feelings.

Step 2. Seek Support:

No person is an island. We all need the comforting embrace of community, the listening ear of a friend, or the guiding hand of a mentor, especially when we face setbacks. After the scam, the weight of the ordeal could feel heavy, almost suffocating. But remember, carrying this burden alone isn't an indication of strength.

Seeking support signifies strength. It's an acknowledgment that healing and recovery are collaborative processes. Humans are wired for connection, and it is through these connections that we find solace, understanding, and encouragement.

When you share your story, you not only lighten your heart but also become a shining example for others who might be going through similar struggles. They might not have faced a scam, but the emotional aftermath—the feelings of betrayal, the shattered trust—these are universal. By seeking support, you create a space where experiences are shared, lessons are learned, and healing begins.

Tips & Advice:

Professional Help: There's no shame in seeking therapy or counseling. Professionals can provide coping strategies, offer a fresh perspective, and facilitate healing.

Support Groups: These are communities of individuals who've faced similar situations. Sharing and listening in such a space can be profoundly therapeutic.

Open up to Loved Ones: Friends and family might not fully understand what you went through, but they can offer comfort, love, and a shoulder to lean on.

Avoid Isolation: Even if you're not ready to talk, surround yourself with positive influences. Attend social gatherings, join clubs, or participate in community events.

Educate Yourself: Understanding the nature of scams and their impact can help in healing. Attend workshops or seminars that address these topics, connecting you with experts and other survivors.

Life's setbacks, like scams, aren't just about the loss of tangible assets; they rob us of our trust, confidence, and peace. Yet, with self-awareness and a supportive community, we can reclaim not just what was lost but also discover newfound wisdom, strength, and purpose.

Step 3. Embrace Learning:

Facing setbacks is an inevitable part of the human journey. However, the difference between those who remain stuck in their misfortunes and those who rise above them often boils down to how they use the faculties of the mind. One of those intellectual faculties is that perception will make all the difference in your climb. By choosing to view setbacks as opportunities for growth and embracing the learning that comes with them, we transform our struggles into stepping stones.

In the aftermath of the scam, it would have been easy to succumb to feelings of regret and self-blame. However, with a shift in perspective, this unfortunate event became a powerful lesson. Every experience, good or bad, carries a lesson. In this case, it was about the importance of vigilance in the digital age, the need to establish personal boundaries, and to recognize the signs of manipulation.

Tips & Advice:

Maintain a Growth Mindset: Believe in the ability to grow and change. Instead of thinking, "I'm a failure," consider, "What can this teach me?"

Document Lessons: Whenever you face a challenge, write down what it taught you. This can serve as a guide for future challenges.

Seek Knowledge: Read books, attend seminars, or take courses on topics that empower you. Knowledge not only prevents past mistakes but paves the way for future successes.

Challenge Yourself: Put your lessons into practice. Set small challenges for yourself to apply what you've learned.

Share Your Learnings: Teaching others can solidify your own understanding and turn your past ordeal into a role model for others.

Step 4. Practice Resilience & Set Clear Goals:

Resilience is the art of bouncing back. It's not about avoiding falls but rising each time we fall, stronger and wiser. The scam experience, devastating as it was, provided an opportunity to build this invaluable trait. Resilience doesn't mean forgetting the pain or bypassing the healing process. Instead, it's about integrating the experience, learning from it, and moving forward with renewed vigor. Setting clear goals is paramount. Knowing where you're at and where you're going is needed to carve the path moving forward.

True resilience is developed in the crucible of adversity. It's the small choices we make daily: the choice to get out of bed, to reach out for support, to confront rather than avoid our feelings, and to believe in tomorrow's promise. It's the understanding that storms, no matter how fierce, eventually pass and often leave behind clear skies and fresher air.

Tips & Advice:

Acknowledge Your Feelings: It's okay to feel pain, grief, or anger. Give yourself permission to feel, but don't let these emotions dictate your actions.

Celebrate Small Wins: Every step forward, no matter how small, is a victory. Celebrate it.

Stay Connected: Being surrounded by supportive people can significantly bolster resilience. They remind us of our worth and capabilities even when we forget.

Maintain a Routine: In tumultuous times, a routine can offer a sense of normalcy and purpose.

Set Clear Goals: Knowing where you're heading can give direction and purpose to your actions. Break down big goals into manageable steps and tackle them one at a time.

Self-Care: Prioritize activities that rejuvenate your mind, body, and spirit. Whether it's a hobby, exercise, or meditation, ensure you carve out time for self-renewal.

Embracing learning and practicing resilience aren't just tools to overcome setbacks; they're foundational principles for a fulfilled life. They allow us to navigate life's unpredictable waters with grace, courage, and unwavering hope. By cultivating these traits, not only do we recover from adversities, but often find ourselves on higher ground than where we began.

Step 5. Set Healthy Boundaries:

Boundaries are the invisible lines we draw around ourselves to protect our energy, well-being, and peace of mind. When we fail to establish these protective barriers, we become vulnerable to external influences, often leading to feelings of being overwhelmed, exploited, or mistreated. Set boundaries as you attempt your deliberate climb.

Reflecting on the scam incident, it becomes evident how a lack of clear boundaries allowed an external entity to exploit and harm. Setting boundaries isn't about shutting the world out, but ensuring you interact with it on your terms, guarding your emotional and mental space.

Tips & Advice:

Self-Reflection: Start by understanding your needs, values, and limits. Know what you can tolerate and what makes you feel uncomfortable or stressed.

Communicate Clearly: Once you've recognized your boundaries, express them directly and clearly to those around you.

Practice Saying 'No': Remember, 'No' is a complete sentence. You don't owe anyone an explanation for safeguarding your well-being.

Seek Mutual Respect: Surround yourself with people who understand and respect your boundaries. Distance yourself from those who consistently violate them.

Reassess Regularly: Life changes and so might your boundaries. It's crucial to check in with yourself regularly to ensure they're still serving you.

Step 6. Harness the Power of Surrender:

There's a common misconception that surrendering means giving up. It's about recognizing that there are forces larger than us at play, understanding the limitations of our control, and allowing life to unfold with trust. The experience of being scammed could evoke feelings of anger, betrayal, and a burning desire to regain control. Yet, in that space of chaos, surrender can be the calm anchor.

By surrendering, you acknowledge the situation, accept the feelings it brings, and make a conscious choice not to let it define you. It's the realization that even in the storm's eye, there's a quiet place within where peace resides.

Tips & Advice:

Acknowledge Reality: It's essential to recognize and accept the situation for what it is without any sugarcoating or denial.

Detach from the Outcome: While it's natural to hope for specific results, releasing attachment to them reduces anxiety and disappointment.

Trust in the Process: Understand that everything unfolds as it should. Even hardships carry hidden lessons.

Stay Present: Instead of dwelling on past mistakes or future uncertainties, ground yourself in the present moment.

Seek Higher Guidance: Whether through meditation, prayer, or simply introspection, connecting with a higher source can provide clarity and solace.

Remember, surrendering doesn't signify weakness. Instead, it's a potent tool that allows us to find serenity amidst chaos. Similarly, setting healthy boundaries doesn't mean shutting out love or opportunities, but ensuring that we interact with the world in ways that nurture and respect our inherent worth. By mastering these principles, we not only safeguard our well-being but also pave the way for more authentic and meaningful connections.

Step 7. Establish Order:

Life, with its unexpected twists and turns, can often feel chaotic. However, even amidst this unpredictability, establishing order can be your anchor, guiding you through challenges with a clear mind and structured approach. My experience with the scam is a vivid illustration of life's disorder. Yet, by instilling order in various facets of my life, I can navigate crises with more clarity and confidence.

Tips & Advice:

Routine Is Key: Start and end your day with a set routine. This predictability can bring comfort during tumultuous times.

Prioritize Tasks: Focus on what's essential. List tasks and tackle them based on urgency and importance.

Declutter Regularly: Whether it's your workspace or home, organized surroundings often lead to an organized mind. Remove what doesn't serve you.

Time Management: Allocate specific times for specific tasks. This prevents feeling overwhelmed and boosts productivity.

Stay Grounded: When chaos unfolds, take deep breaths, and remind yourself of your ability to handle situations systematically.

Step 8. Nurture Emotional Resilience:

Emotional resilience is the ability to bounce back from adversities, to heal, and to continue moving forward. My scam ordeal was a stark confrontation with vulnerability, betrayal, and loss. Yet, as the narrative of my story unfolds, the cultivation of emotional resilience stands out as a shining star, illuminating the path out of despair.

Tips & Advice:

Accept Your Emotions: Don't suppress your feelings. It's okay to feel hurt, betrayed, or broken. Acknowledge these emotions without judgment.

Reframe Your Perspective: Instead of viewing adversities as insurmountable problems, see them as challenges to overcome or lessons to learn.

Build a Support System: Surround yourself with loved ones, friends, or professionals who can offer understanding, advice, or just a listening ear.

Engage in Self-Care: Prioritize activities that relax and rejuvenate you. Whether it's reading, meditation, exercise, or any other activity, self-care boosts emotional strength.

Celebrate Small Victories: Every hurdle you overcome, no matter how tiny, demonstrates your strength. Acknowledge and celebrate these moments.

Emotional resilience isn't just about surviving challenges; it's about thriving despite them. Similarly, establishing order isn't about curbing spontaneity but building a foundation that allows spontaneity to flourish without leading to chaos. Both these principles, when practiced, can transform setbacks into setups for triumphant comebacks.

Step 9. Serve Others:

One of the most transformative realizations in life is understanding that our experiences, as challenging as they might be, can serve as beacons of hope and guidance for others. In the aftermath of my scam ordeal, the inclination might have been to close off, to shield my heart from further pain. But by turning that pain into a mission to serve others, I've exemplified the redemptive power of service.

Tips & Advice:

Share Your Story: Your experiences, while unique, can resonate with many. By sharing your journey, you offer solace and insights to those in similar situations.

Volunteer: Lend your time and skills to organizations or causes that resonate with you. This can not only bring a sense of purpose, but also foster a community of like-minded individuals.

Teach: Turn your experiences into lessons for others. Whether it's a workshop, an online course, or casual mentorship, your wisdom can guide you.

Practice Random Acts of Kindness: Sometimes, small acts can have the most significant impact. Offer a smile, help a stranger, or simply listen. You never know whose day you might turn around.

Stay Open: Keep your heart open to the needs of those around you. Service isn't always about grand gestures; often, it's about being present and available.

Step 10. Embrace Kindness & Empathy:

Life's challenges, like the scam I endured, can sometimes harden hearts, making walls seem like the only protective measure. However, true healing and growth stem from kindness and empathy—not just towards others but towards oneself. When we extend understanding and gentleness, even in the face of betrayal, we not only elevate our own spirit but inspire those around us.

Tips & Advice:

Self-Compassion: Before extending kindness to others, practice it with yourself. Recognize your worth and give yourself the grace to heal and grow.

Active Listening: When someone shares, truly listen. Offer them a safe space to express without judgment.

Avoid Assumptions: Every individual is fighting their own battle. Instead of making assumptions, approach situations with a desire to understand.

Express Gratitude: Recognize and appreciate the kindness shown to you. A simple 'thank you' can uplift you and the other person.

Educate & Advocate: Promote kindness and empathy actively. Whether it's through community engagements, conversations, or online platforms, be a voice that champions understanding and compassion.

In serving others, we often find a deeper sense of purpose, understanding that our pain can have profound meaning when channeled positively. Similarly, by embracing kindness and empathy, we recognize the interconnectedness of our journeys, choosing love and understanding over resentment and isolation. These principles, when adopted, not only heal scars but lay the foundation for a life of richness and fulfillment.

Step 11. Re-establish Goals:

Life's setbacks, such as the scam I experienced, often create a rift between where we are and where we thought we'd be. The path, once clear, becomes muddled with doubt and uncertainty. But remember, every setback is a setup for a comeback. While the path may have changed, the destination can still remain the same or perhaps even evolve into something grander. It all begins by reestablishing your goals.

Tips & Advice:

Reflect on Your Why: Before setting new goals, understand your underlying motivations. Why did you set these goals in the first place? Has the 'why' changed?

Break It Down: Large goals can feel overwhelming. Break them down into smaller, manageable steps. Each step you accomplish brings you closer to the bigger picture.

Set Big Goals: Ensure your goals are Specific, Measurable, Achievable, Relevant, and Time-bound. This clarity helps in charting out a definitive path forward.

Stay Flexible: Understand that goals can evolve. Be open to reevaluating and adjusting them based on your growth and changing circumstances.

Seek Accountability: Share your goals with someone you trust—a friend, family member, or mentor. Their encouragement and accountability can be invaluable.

Step 12. Celebrate Your Journey:

It's easy to become fixated on destinations—the end goals. But the journey, with its highs and lows, struggles, and triumphs, is where the true magic lies. My scam ordeal wasn't a detour from my story; it was a chapter that added depth and dimension to my narrative. And every chapter, every step, every hurdle overcome deserves to be celebrated.

Tips & Advice:

Document Your Progress: Keep a journal or a record of your milestones, no matter how small. Reflecting on how far you've come can be a powerful motivator.

Reward Yourself: Every accomplishment, even a tiny one, is significant. Treat yourself when you achieve a milestone, reminding yourself of the effort you've put in.

Share Your Story: Just as you are doing with this book, share your journey with others. Your resilience can be an inspiration for many.

Practice Gratitude: Often, it's the challenges that teach us the most. Be grateful for every experience, for they have molded you into the person you are today.

Embrace Every Emotion: The journey is made up of a myriad of emotions—joy, pain, hope, despair. Celebrate every emotion, knowing it's all part of the beautiful tapestry of life.

In reestablishing your goals, you chart a renewed path filled with purpose and direction. And by celebrating your journey, you not only honor your growth, but also inspire countless others to find strength in their stories. The climb, as they say, is tough, but the view from the top is worth every step.

AFTERWORD: THE "DELIBERATE" SHIFT

So, let me take you back to a turning point in my life. Picture this: I'm on the Gold Coast, Australia, standing at the base of the Q1 Tower. Yep, the same tower that was the world's tallest residential building for a while. I had friends—Mark and Michelle—cheering me on, and a crazy idea to climb this beast. Why? To face my fear of heights head-on.

Man, was it terrifying! Every step up that 322.5-meter monster felt like a deliberate dance with fear. A few times, I even thought of turning back. But then, in those quiet pauses, my goals whispered to me. And with sweaty palms and a racing heart, I kept climbing. You know when they say the view is better at the top? They weren't kidding. Standing there, this book's title, "The Deliberate Climb," just came to me. All my ups and downs, every twist and turn—it all felt... deliberate.

Here's what I've noticed: so many people are walking through life like they're asleep. Their past mistakes and fears? Those have taken the wheel. It's as if they're on autopilot, letting past conditioning and self-limiting beliefs steer them away from a life of abundance. It's heartbreaking to see folks chained to hurtful relationships or letting their feelings and situations decide their destiny, all because they're living unconsciously.

Enter the Deliberate Movement. Think of it as a mindset shift, a life-changing perspective that can light up every moment of every day. It's all about conscious choice. About grabbing the wheel of your life back from past mistakes and regrets. Remember, no matter where you're at right now or what you're grappling with, you can change your story. Heck, you can rewrite entire chapters! All it takes is a deliberate step.

And ladies, I see you. The world can sometimes be a tough place for women. Cultural expectations, self-doubt, and external pressures can weigh heavy. But I firmly believe that empowering women can shake up entire communities. So, if you or a woman you know is battling a setback, dive deeper. Check out the resources at ***www.naisesilapa.com.*** We're building a Deliberate Academy, aiming to empower women to be unapologetically deliberate in every aspect of their lives.

In conclusion, we all face storms. But remember this: every crisis is an invitation. An invite to become more resilient, to grow. Whatever you're facing, let this book be your guidepost on your deliberate journey. And if you're itching to dive deeper, there's a fantastic 26-week Thinking into Results course waiting for you at ***www.naisesilapa.com.*** Here's to deliberate choices and brighter tomorrows! ✸

ACKNOWLEDGMENTS

In the intricate tapestry of life's journey, we are held aloft by the threads of love, support, and guidance from those around us. This book is not only a product of my experiences, but also a reflection of the unwavering support I've received from many.

My mother, Oloa Amosa Faamatuainu, was a reservoir of love and understanding during my darkest days. Her intuitive presence and boundless love for her family have been the guiding lights of my life. Her spirit continues to inspire and guide me every day.

My heartfelt love and appreciation go to my children, Symon (and partner Tegan), Joshua, and Monique, who have been my pillars of strength. Your unconditional love and support have been my sanctuary, providing me with the courage to face life's challenges. To my grandchildren, Mathias, Leilani, and Mahalia, you are my inspiration.

To my sister, Hana, and her husband, Pastor Joe, you have been profound sources of inspiration. Your kindness and support have not gone unnoticed. To my nephews, Tum, Sam, and Simeona, witnessing your growth and success has been a great source of hope and pride.

Special thanks to my nephew, Hooligan Hefs, for his profound contribution to my book. Hefs, your journey through life's ups and downs and your success as a rapper deeply inspire me. Writing the foreword for *The Deliberate Climb,* you've added a layer of authenticity that resonates with many. Your story is an example of courage and creativity, and your support in my endeavor is invaluable. Thank you for your encouragement and for being a guiding star for the youth.

A huge thank you to my brothers, Sam Faala and Amosa, for their support, inspiration, and amazing help with moving homes. Their strength, wisdom, and solid support made everything easier, guiding us with love and patience.

I'm deeply grateful to my cousins and extended family for your unwavering support and encouragement. Your faith in me and the strength of our family bonds have been a source of fortitude in challenging times.

To my cherished friends, Mark O'Toole and Michelle Lee, your unwavering support, wise counsel, and the inspiration you provided for the Q1 climb have been instrumental in my journey of personal growth. I am deeply grateful for your companionship and the strength you have lent me in times of need, not to mention my gratitude for the car you lent me when I couldn't afford to fix my car.

A special acknowledgment to Dr. Cassandra J. O'Loughlin, whose wisdom as an author and editor has been invaluable in shaping this book. Cassandra, your love, support, and insightful feedback have been essential in bringing my story to life. Your contributions have not gone unnoticed.

I am indebted to the enlightening teachings of Bob Proctor and Maxwell Maltz, which have illuminated my path.

To my friend Shelly Southam, whose understanding and empathy have been a source of light in my life. Your presence has provided me with comfort and strength. Thank you for being more than just a friend; thank you for being a pillar of support and cherished confidant.

To everyone who has been a part of this journey—friends, church sisters, therapists, support groups, colleagues, and the professionals at Hasmark Publishing who helped turn my vision into reality—your contributions have made this journey richer and more meaningful.

And to you, the reader, for joining me in this exploration of resilience and triumph, thank you. Your engagement and growth are the ultimate testament to the power of this story.

ABOUT THE AUTHOR

Born in the vibrant islands of Samoa and now residing in Australia, Naise is a beacon of resilience and transformation. A single mother of three and a doting grandmother to three, she embodies the spirit of unwavering strength and dedication. Her journey from the simple island life to the dynamic world of Australia in 1985 has been nothing short of remarkable.

With an academic background in human services and counseling, Naise has dedicated over two decades of her career to the banking sector and counseling, bringing financial acumen and emotional intelligence to the forefront of her work. Currently, she serves the public while also thriving as an entrepreneur, a property investor, and a consultant in the personal development field, specifically as a Proctor Gallagher Consultant.

Her book, *The Deliberate Climb,* is not just a narration of her life's adversities, but a testament to her indomitable spirit. From surviving a scam that stripped her of everything to overcoming emotional and financial manipulation, health scares, and a traumatic car accident, Naise's life is a narrative of fighting back and soaring higher. Her experiences in a culture that traditionally silenced the voices of the young and the traumatic conditioning of her childhood have only fueled her passion to guide others towards self-discovery and resilience.

A lover of nature, Naise finds solace in hiking, bushwalking, and embracing the outdoors. Her commitment to a healthy lifestyle, coupled with her deep-rooted faith in God, underscores her holistic approach to wellness. As a voracious reader and a seeker of Divine downloads, she fills her life with positivity, constantly seeking to grow and inspire.

In *The Deliberate Climb,* Naise shares not just her journey, but also the universal lessons of hope, faith, and the power of a renewed mindset. It is her aspiration that readers facing adversities will find solace and strength in her words, connect with their true selves, and harness the laws of the Universe to realize their dreams. For Naise, success is not a secret but a system, a belief firmly rooted in the power of positive thinking, self-love, and unwavering faith.

THINKING INTO RESULTS PROGRAM

This exceptionally designed program is presented in 12 relevant, simple, and practical lessons to ensure that the success mindset becomes a part of each person's thinking and actions. This leads to the results the person wants most in life.

Thinking Into Results addresses the root cause of success . . .

1. **The Power of Immediate Transformation**

    The moment you begin to activate your consciousness on dual levels, your mind starts to absorb and react dynamically. We guide you every step of the way.

2. **The Strength of Consistent Reinforcement**

    Across a span of 24 weeks, you'll delve into the profound impact of repetition. This systematic approach ensures you cultivate habits that pave the way to enduring abundance and prosperity.

3. **Mastery for a Lifetime**

    Empower yourself with an everlasting ability to attain any aspiration. With this program, you gain an unwavering capability to manifest your desires in any facet of life. Click the link below to learn more.

https://naisesilapa.com/thinking-into-results-program/

Website - www.naisesilapa.com

Instagram - www.instagram.com/naisesilapa

Email - naise@naisesilapa.com

www.ingramcontent.com/pod-product-compliance
Lightning Source LLC
LaVergne TN
LVHW051519070426
835507LV00023B/3199